Custom Automotive & Motorcycle Airbrushing

MODERN METHODS AND SECRETS REVEALED

by
Pamela Shanteau
and Donn Shanteau

About the Author

Pamela Shanteau has been airbrushing since 1976, when she started out as PK Custom Airbrushing. In 1984 she married Donn Shanteau, and the two teamed to operate Air Illusions Inc., in Swanton, Ohio. Over the years she has airbrushed for celebrities and serious car and motorcycle builders, in addition to the average guy or gal who desired an eye-popping paint job.

Pamela's art has been published in dozens of custom-vehicle magazines and calendars, including the first-ever Iwata airbrush calendar in 2006, as well as the 2006 BASF RM paint calendar.

Donn acts as the Scotty to Pam's Captain Kirk. He pushes the buttons and pulls the levers to keep their ship operational. With Donn working in the capacities of webmaster, photographer and business agent, Pam is free to be creative and concentrate on her current assignment.

Donn and Pamela Shanteau
Air Illusions Airbrushing
13810 County Road 4-1
Swanton, Ohio 43558
www.pamelashanteau.com

Custom Automotive & Motorcycle Airbrushing 101: Methods and Secrets Revealed. Copyright © 2006 by Pamela Shanteau. Manufactured in the United States. All rights reserved. No part of this book may be reproduced in any form or by any electronic or mechanical means, including information storage and retrieval systems without permission in writing from the publisher, except by a reviewer, who may quote brief passages in a review. Published by Iwata-Medea, 79 SE Taylor, Portland, Oregon 97202 USA. (503) 253-7308. First edition.

Library of Congress Control Number: 2007922288
ISBN 13# 978-0-9671643-1-1
ISBN# 0-9671643-1-1
Printed in China by Crown Media & Printing, Inc. 1+877.777.9392
Shanteau, Pamela
    Custom Automotive & Motorcycle Airbrushing 101: Methods and Secrets
    Revealed / by Pamela Shanteau . — 1st ed.
Co-Author; Donn Shanteau
Design by A. D. Cook dba ADCook Inc. - online at ADCook.com
Edited by Zookeeper, LLC. - online at Zookeeper.com
All photos by Donn "Too Tall" Shanteau unless otherwise noted. Airbrush and air gun images on pages 31-33 & 35 provided by Iwata-Medea Inc. Used by permission.

The Iwata-Medea logo, Iwata-Medea®, Iwata Kustom™, Iwata Micron™, Power Jet Pro™, Power Jet™, Power Jet Lite™, Medea Super Lube™, and all products denoted with ® or ™ are registered trademarks or trademarks of Iwata-Medea Inc. • Iwata® and the Iwata logo are registered trademarks of Anest Iwata Japan • All other trademarks are of their respective owners. For more information visit iwata-medea.com

Acknowledgements

Thanks to BASF and Iwata-Medea for their staunch support and belief in my abilities. Great products make for superior results.

William "Bill" Watkins
Watkins Auto Body
6930 Airport Hwy.
Holland, Ohio

Bill's expert paint and clear-coat work make my airbrushing look its best.

Thanks also to Roeder Harley-Davidson (Sandusky, Ohio), Toledo Harley-Davidson (Toledo, Ohio) and Signature Harley-Davidson (Perrysburg, Ohio) for your continued goodwill and friendship.

A.D. Cook — A.D. Cook has always been on my list of "Airbrush Heroes," so it was a true honor for me to have him design and edit this book. We share a kinship in the fact that his background in the "Arts" shows in everything he paints and he paints in multiple mediums. Because he is very proficient in every airbrush application that he has an interest in pursuing, A.D.'s mural, metal and fine art paintings are a joy to behold. I still think that he paints chrome effects as well as anyone in the world. Because he develops his own original ideas and images for his paintings, his style is unique, identifiable and technically correct.

Having someone with A.D.'s high standards as an editor was a little scary; since he is not an "Easy Pleaser," so I am very happy that we passed the audition. ☺

Thanks to A.D. and Kathryn Cook for all their effort to make this book the best it can be!

Craig Fraser — Craig has been an airbrushing icon for decades. Most probably, no one in the world has more published articles on the subject. His technical knowledge of paints and additives combined with his considerable painting skills make him a top-shelf Kustom painter. His writing skills and airbrushing experience also make him a wonderful teacher/mentor to thousands of airbrush neophytes. I was very pleased when Craig took time away from his business "Air Syndicate" to write the forward for this book. Having the "Mad Ambassador" of airbrushing co-sign our book is a good thing, since Craig is no push-over when it comes to appraising airbrush painting techniques and disseminating information. If Craig likes it….you'll like it. Thanks for everything Craig, Paint on Dude!

Table of Contents

FORWARD / INTRODUCTION

— Page 6 —

CHAPTER ONE

Auto-Shop Requirements

— Page 11 —

CHAPTER TWO

Auto-Painting Accessories

— Page 19 —

CHAPTER THREE

Paints & Additives

— Page 27 —

CHAPTER FOUR

Airbrush / Air Gun Choices

—Page 31 —

CHAPTER FIVE

Airbrush / Air Gun Operation

— Page 35 —

CHAPTER SIX

Masking Methods

— Page 51 —

CHAPTER SEVEN

Ace of Spades Skeleton Lesson

— 61 —

CHAPTER EIGHT

Tiger Bike Lesson

— Page 79 —

CHAPTER NINE

Ghost King Lesson

— Page 91 —

CHAPTER TEN

Draco Exercise

— Page 105 —

CHAPTER ELEVEN

Gallery

— Page 141 —

CHAPTER TWELVE

Other Works

— Page 149 —

GLOSSARY / TROUBLESHOOTING / RESOURCES

— Page 154 —

Forward

In the ocean of Kustom paint "how-to" books that have been flooding the market, it is nice to see one that stands out in the crowd. I have been writing articles on Kustom painting for well over a decade, so I am a bit picky when it comes to the tech stuff.

Pam did it right by focusing on the basics. She also allowed her own unique style from her fine art background to come through. Writing about Kustom painting is similar to the actual art of Kustom painting. It is a balance. Pam hit the nail on the head by offering a book that is very much about her perspective on the industry, as well as catering to the techniques that many painters want to see. The book is progressive in nature: It starts out slowly and methodically, with the basics, and as the book progresses, the demos become more intricate, with the gallery of finished work at the end.

I have known Pam and Donn Shanteau for years, and they have been one of the great educational teams in airbrushing, traveling across the country teaching hands-on workshops for Iwata/Medea/Artool. Pam managed to take her hands-on workshop experience and put it into print form. Their book is not only a great "kick-start" for the absolute beginner, but has enough advanced techniques and tricks to entertain even the most jaded veteran. I like that I can see Pam's past illustration experience and fine art techniques come through in the demos.

While many books cover only the artistic techniques used in painting, Pam has included numerous chapters that cover the nuts and bolts part of the industry. From equipment choices, to materials, to shop set-up, this book covers it all. Besides having plenty of color pictures to make the book an interesting coffee-table piece, it also has more than enough information to back up the fact that it is, after all, an educational tool for "Kustomizers." Enjoy the read.

Paint to live, live to paint,
Craig Fraser — Air Syndicate Inc., Bakersfield, CA

Introduction

Donn and Pam Shanteau

Over the last three decades, automotive and motorcycle custom painting have undergone quite a transformation. What was once done in relative seclusion is now in the mainstream of the entertainment industry.

Cable television has been fertile soil for the cultivation of entertaining and informative programs relating to custom cars and motorcycles. The finishing touch on these televised custom creations is, of course, the paint. Everyone wants to make their own statement with their vehicles, from the wheels to the paint. This has created an avid demand for qualified custom vehicle painters worldwide. Due to the extreme media exposure, some custom painters have become celebrities in their own right.

Any competent airbrush painter, regardless of artistic talent, can earn an above-average income with the right skills. By utilizing the painting aids and accessories that are available today, novices can get great results with a little practice.

While there are many ways to earn money with the airbrush, automotive painting is currently the most lucrative. Making the transition from airbrushing or painting in other mediums to custom auto and cycle painting is not too difficult with guidance and good information. That is what this book is all about.

As I share my decades of custom painting experience, you will have the information you need to effectively enter the custom airbrushing and painting industry and be successful.

How did I get started custom painting? My first hands-on experience with the airbrush was the result of a dare.

Since I was a small child, I knew that I wanted to be an artist. There was no ambiguity in my mind. I was going to be an artist, and that was that. Almost all of my high school and college classes focused on art. Once I was in college, I was not drawn to painting so much as 3-D forms. I envisioned that gem cutting, metal sculpture and glass blowing would be my means of income. I never realized that I would not be earning my living by creating 3-D objects, but by painting on them.

Upon leaving school and making a first foray into the workforce, I realized that there wasn't much demand for a gem cutter or metal sculptor in the farmlands of northwest Ohio. In need of immediate income, I wandered into a custom car-restoration shop that was taking applications for a secretary. I told the owner that I didn't type and didn't know much about cars, but I knew a little about metal work and I could draw. After everyone stopped laughing, they went back to work airbrushing a stripe on a Triumph Spitfire sports car.

The painting process they were using intrigued me. After one side of the hood was done, I mentioned that it looked easy and I probably could do it. I endured another round of laughter at my expense. With a big grin, the shop owner offered me the airbrush and a challenge: "Little girlie, you are welcome to give it a try if you think it's so easy." He leaned back in his chair and gave me a one-minute primer on airbrush operation. I don't know if I was ever so nervous. To everyone's surprise (including my own), I duplicated the stripe on the other side of the hood to the painter's satisfaction.

Later that week I began painting pinstripes and other simple designs on the custom hot rods and other exotic cars that the shop restored. After about six months of practicing on my own at home, I decided to open my own shop and began marketing my airbrush services all over northwest Ohio and eventually the entire U.S.A.

Over the ensuing years I took advantage of any airbrush-related publications that became available to expand my painting skills. Attending airbrushing seminars provided an opportunity to meet fellow painters and continue to augment my airbrushing skills.

The payoff for this effort is a successful custom-airbrushing business and international notoriety from my work being published in magazines and calendars that are seen worldwide. Many cars and motorcycles that I have airbrushed compete at the highest levels. Their performance showcases my airbrushing to other top-notch builders who might require a competent airbrush artist.

My husband Donn and I wrote *The Ultimate Airbrush Handbook* for Watson-Guptill Publishing in 2002. It explains basic and intermediate airbrush techniques and applies them to a myriad of projects. Thousands of readers worldwide have benefited from the information it contains. I have taught airbrushing to thousands of students in association with the United Auto Workers Union (UAW), United Steel Workers Union, Michigan Dept. of Rehabilitation and the United States Veterans Administration. Information about dates and locations of workshops hosted by myself or other entities can be found on my web site, www.pamelashanteau.com

For this book, I am painting a series of aluminum panels with a skull/skeleton playing card theme. I will explain the techniques used to paint them to help you understand how to duplicate the effects and create your own airbrushed art on vehicles.

I will also demonstrate a tiger skin themed motorcycle mural on a motorcycle tank and fender set to demonstrate how to work on curved surfaces.

While the airbrushed images that appear in this book might seem too complicated to tackle, they are all created by combining the most elemental airbrush strokes, the dot, the line and the gradation or color fade. Learn these basic techniques and you are sure to succeed with your airbrushing adventures.

Paint Long and Prosper,

Pamela Shanteau

CHAPTER ONE

Auto-Shop Requirements

Creating the optimal workspace requires some consideration. First, determine if you will offer complete paint services or specialty custom painting only.

Complete paint service means that you would do everything from vehicle disassembly and painting to the final clear coat and re-assembly. Specialty custom painting focuses only on the art or graphics that are incorporated into the complete paint job. Both approaches are viable business models and require the same basic items. The difference between the two is a matter of scale.

Automotive paint vendors, or "jobbers," not only sell paint but most of the accessories and essentials mentioned below. You will likely find a paint jobber in your area by looking in the phone book under *Automobile Repairing and Service* or *Automobile Paint/Painting Supply* or similar heading. Every telephone directory has its own listing system, so you may have to search a bit to find the correct heading. Once you develop a relationship with your local paint supplier, you will discover that they have a wealth of information available for the asking. They will gladly answer any specific questions you have about any of the products that they sell.

Shop Set-Up for Specialty Custom Painting.

I am definitely a specialty painter, because I want to concentrate on what I do best; create art. I do not regularly apply primer paints, base paints or clear coats at our shop. All of these processes require extensive sanding and time-consuming labor that frankly is not very artistic and is very dirty work. Therefore, we subcontract every part of the painting process that is not directly related to rendering images or lettering. We have developed a small cadre of trusted painters that operate their own businesses in the area and we trust them to do their part of the job with the quality our customers expect.

I regularly go off-site to a full-service shop to airbrush anything larger than motorcycle or car parts. Once my part of the job is completed, the shop guys spray the clear coat and polish and buff the clear coat to a smooth, shiny finish. They are happy to have the extra work and I am happy to move on to the next assignment.

Efficient shop set-up saves money.

I do most of my work out of a small 24 x 36 ft. shop located on the property where I reside. This shop is an efficient size to use either an airbrush or larger air gun to paint artwork or lettering on my clients' vehicles. The workspace is also perfect for small items, such as motorcycle parts and helmets. The lack of overhead and the convenience of location make this a feel-good workspace for me and my checkbook.

Here is a list of the shop essentials required to set up for specialty painting.

- **Exhaust Fan.** Make sure to install a fan that has the capacity to pull any over-spray that you might generate out of the building. Generally, the fan is wall mounted. I use a squirrel cage-type fan in my shop. Paddle fans of various capacities also work well.

Paddle-style exhaust fan

- **Assortment of Air Guns and Airbrushes.** You will want at least one air gun each in the large, medium and small sizes. I prefer the high volume - low pressure (HVLP) guns. They produce much less over-spray than traditional spray guns. Your air guns should be able to spray pattern diameters from 12 down to 2 inches.

Mid-size spray guns are important too. An excellent choice, and my personal favorite, is the Anest Iwata RG-3.

The same logic applies to your airbrush selection. You should own airbrushes with paint-nozzle sizes from .5 mm to .18 mm. They are capable of rendering patterns from 2 inches down to a hair's width.

Iwata has a wonderful line of airbrushes designed specifically for automotive applications. The Kustom series airbrushes are uniquely outfitted for urethanes and automotive finishes.

- **5 HP Oil-less Compressor with a 30-40 Gallon Air Tank.** This size works well with large spray guns and is more than adequate for airbrushing. If I must move the compressor off-site, it can be laid down for transport, due to its oil-less design.

Assorted Tips & Words of Wisdom

Good music can make the day special. Long hours of fashioning stencils or painting mega-amounts of dagger strokes to create a fur covered motorcycle can be tedious; I listen to everything from Punk to Monk, but I like Pink Floyd and Janis Joplin the best.

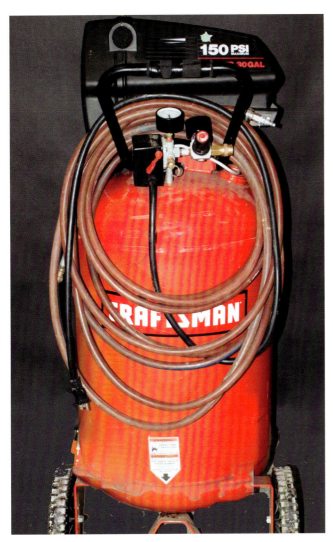

5 hp 30 gallon oil-less compressor

air manifold. They are a must-have time and labor-saving convenience.

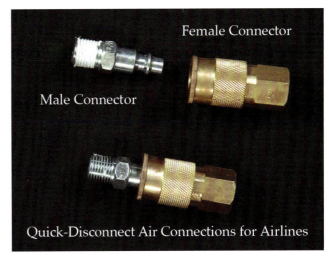

Male and female quick disconnects

My big compressor is located in a building adjacent to my shop, and the compressed air is piped into the shop air distribution system through a wall. The air system must have a moisture trap/filter and be regulated so the air pressure can be adjusted. An oil-vapor filter installed in the air system is also desirable if your air compressor uses oil. The oil vapor separator can be mounted on the compressor. The moisture trap and regulator should be near your work station where they can be adjusted and maintained. Make sure to get enough air line to circumnavigate your shop.

Better for smaller jobs is the Power Jet Lite or Power Jet Pro from Iwata Medea.

- **Quick-disconnect Fittings.** Use this type of fitting to attach air lines to the compressor or air manifold. They are a must-have time and labor-saving convenience.

- **Work Tables/Surfaces.** Cabinets and counters that once resided in my kitchen have been recycled into paint-supply storage. The countertop serves as a paint-mixing table and stencil-burning station. Two tables that are six feet long and 30 inches wide give me plenty of room for the parts that I am painting. Additional tables line my walls to hold parts awaiting paint. When I need more table space, I like to use four-foot-long folding tables with a rigid plastic top. Some models offer adjustable legs that make it easy to work on parts while standing up. Another added benefit is that the plastic tops will not easily scratch the parts during the course of the paint job.

- **Lighting.** Color-correct fluorescent lighting is recommended. Position the lights so your painting area is well-lit from every angle. Usually more light is better, especially when painting finely detailed designs.

- **Climate Control.** You will want a furnace with the capacity to replace the heat pulled from the shop by the exhaust fan. This is a crucial aspect of shop design in colder climates. I use one that draws its air from outside the shop to protect against fire hazards from solvent fumes. An air-conditioner may be required to cool the paint shop and reduce humidity in times of excessive heat – 70-75 degrees Fahrenheit is a good temperature to maintain.

- **Fire.** I have fire extinguishers located at every exit and adjacent to my paint-mixing table. Solvents and their resulting fumes are nothing to fool with. Never allow open flames in the shop.

- **Painter Safety.** Regardless of shop size, the chemicals encountered in the process of automotive painting can be hazardous to your health. Always wear a charcoal respirator or clean-air respirator during the painting process or when mixing paint and cleaning your equipment.

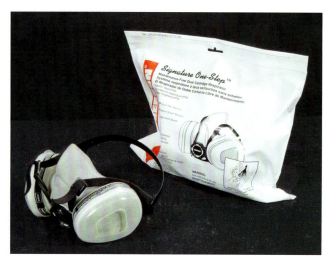

Two-stage charcoal and cotton filter respirator

- **Solvent-Proof Gloves.** These are recommended if your hands have extended contact with the paints or reducers. Eye protection should always be worn when mixing paint, spraying paint and using power tools. Have a well-stocked first-aid kit in plain sight.

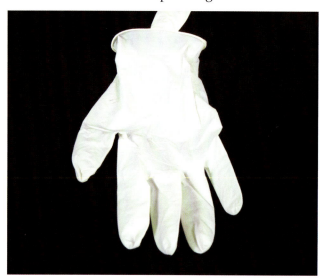

Solvent-proof gloves keep you healthy

Specialty painting has its advantages and disadvantages.

- **Advantages.** I have very few fixed overhead expenses. This is very desirable for a business start-up or any business, for that matter.

Travel expenses, such as car maintenance or fuel, are not an issue. The close proximity of my studios to my residence makes my personal and work schedules flexible. I have no formal business hours that require someone to man the storefront. All customer meetings are by appointment only.

The ambiance is just how I want it. I can work in relative seclusion without any unexpected drop-in customers or sales calls.

A minimal investment in equipment (compared to a full-service shop) was required to set up my shop. In addition to less area to maintain, smaller compressors and air exchange systems can be used for the type of painting that I am doing in-house. No spray booth is required, since I do not spray the base and clear coats. The paint exiting the airbrush dries immediately upon contact with the surface. This makes it possible to paint on work tables in an open shop. The small shop has less area to heat, cool and illuminate. All of these factors add up to a huge savings on both start-up and monthly expenses.

Because all of the dirty work is done off-site, my shop stays quiet and clean.

Shop Set-Up for Full-Service Paint.

A full-service paint shop can repair damaged vehicle parts, and apply primer paint, base-coat paints and clear-coat paints, along with offering airbrushing services. The workspace must be large enough for vehicle storage and disassembly. You will need a good set of tools and a working knowledge of vehicle disassembly.

The process of repairing auto or cycle parts constructed of steel, fiberglass, carbon-fiber or aluminum requires grinding, welding, metal-filler application and a lot of sanding. Needless to say, these activities generate an abundant amount of dust and other contaminants that affect the overall quality of a paint job. *A separate area needs to be designated for these operations*. This will be the dirtiest section of your work area. Avoid tracking the dirt from this area into the painting area.

Establish a painting station or a paint booth equipped with adequate lighting, a regulated compressed-air delivery system, adjustable climate control, paint over-spray ventilation and fire-suppression safety measures. Your painting area should be as insulated from the other sections of the workspace as much as possible to help ensure a flawless finish. Paint booths come in all sizes and shapes. Prices range from a few thousand dollars for a used one to over $100,000 for a state-of-the-art downdraft type paint booth. When the finished paint job leaves a properly maintained downdraft booth, often no polishing or buffing is required, since there are no blemishes in the paint.

Regardless of how clean the paint finish is, I prefer that all of the clear coat applied over my airbrushing be buffed out or "rubbed." This ensures that the final paint exhibits the smoothest finish and highest gloss possible.

Quality paint finishes can be attained without the benefit of a paint booth. Great care must be taken to wet the floor and keep all shop doors closed before, during and after the base- and clear-coat paints are sprayed. Invariably, dust or other imperfections will find their way into the paint. The piece must be wet-sanded with sand-paper 1000 grit or finer to remove these contaminants before moving on to the next paint coat or to the final step, polishing the clear coat to a high gloss.

With attention to detail, a paint job that was done in an open shop can rival the quality of one from an expensive paint booth. The air gun operations in this book take place in an open shop, since this is the most likely set-up for a novice painter.

Once the parts are primed, painted, airbrushed and clear coated, they are usually sanded and buffed to a very smooth finish that displays a high gloss and is devoid of dust flecks or any other undesirable artifact. This buffing can take place in any relatively clean, well-lit environment.

Here is a list of the shop essentials required to set up for full-service painting.

Please note that many of these recommendations are similar to the previously mentioned specialty painting shop. The only difference might be in terms of the capacity of the exhaust fan, heating/cooling system and air system.

- **Exhaust Fan.** Make sure to install a fan that has the capacity to pull any over-spray that you might generate out of the building. Generally, the fan is wall mounted. I use a relatively small squirrel cage-type fan, and it works well for the volume of paint that I spray with the airbrush. Paddle-style fans are a common fixture in most full-service body shops.

- **Assortment of Air Guns and Airbrushes.** You will want at least one air gun each in the large and small size. I prefer the high volume - low pressure (HVLP) guns. They produce much less over-spray than traditional spray guns. Spray pattern diameters should range from 12 inches down to 2 inches. Dedicate one or two spray-guns to spraying only primer paints and a couple of air guns to spraying only clear-coats.

  An assortment of airbrushes with paint nozzle sizes from .5 mm to .18 mm is recommended.

  Mid-size spray guns are important too. An excellent choice, and my personal favorite, is the Anest Iwata RG-3.

  The same logic applies to your airbrush selection. You should own airbrushes with paint-nozzle sizes from .5 mm to .18 mm. They are capable of rendering patterns from 2 inches down to a hair's width.

  Iwata has a wonderful line of airbrushes designed specifically for automotive applications. The Kustom series airbrushes are uniquely outfitted for urethanes and automotive finishes.

- **Air Compressor.** A full-service shop needs a larger air compressor than a specialty shop. A

10 hp or larger compressor with a minimum 60-gallon air storage tank will be needed to power the air tools. Many shops that I work in have compressors in the 35-hp range with a huge 100-gallon-plus air storage tank to keep up with multiple air tools operating at the same time. Air-pressure regulators, and oil-vapor and moisture filters must be installed, as mentioned above in the specialty shop set-up. Don't forget to stock up on air lines to reach from the compressor to your air gun or airbrush line. Get enough air hose to circumnavigate your work area.

Large compressor capable of operating multiple air tools simultaneously

- **Work Tables/Surfaces.** In my opinion, you can't have enough table space. Paint-supply stores sell folding metal stands that support a sheet of plywood. This system works well for portable workbenches. The folding, plastic-top tables mentioned above are also a very good choice for a mobile work surface.

- **Lighting.** Color-correct fluorescent lighting is recommended. Position the lights so your painting area is well-lit from every angle. Usually more light is better when painting finely detailed designs. Keep the lighting consistent in all areas of your shop, so the color you see doesn't change depending on which areas of the shop you are in.

- **Climate Control.** You will want a furnace with the capacity to replace the heat pulled from the shop by the exhaust fan. The larger the fan is, the bigger your furnace needs to be. This is a crucial aspect of shop design in colder climates. I use a furnace that draws its air from outside the shop to protect against fire hazards from solvent fumes being drawn into the combustion chamber. An air conditioner may be required to cool the paint shop and reduce humidity in times of excessive heat – 70-75 degrees Fahrenheit is a good temperature for painting.

- **Fire Safety.** An overhead, automatic fire-suppression system is recommended, particularly in the immediate area of your paint storage, mixing and painting. In the absence of an overhead system, have plenty of chemical fire extinguishers on hand, and train yourself how to use them since there will be no time to read directions if fire breaks out in your shop.

- **Painter Safety.** The chemicals and over-spray encountered in the process of automotive painting can be hazardous to your health. Always wear a respirator during the painting process or when mixing paint and cleaning your equipment to avoid breathing the harmful vapors that are present. Solvent-proof gloves are recommended if your hands have contact with the paints or reducers. Eye protection should always be worn when mixing paint, spraying paint and using power tools. Always have a well-stocked first-aid kit in plain sight. If feasible, an eyewash station is recommended for a full-service shop.

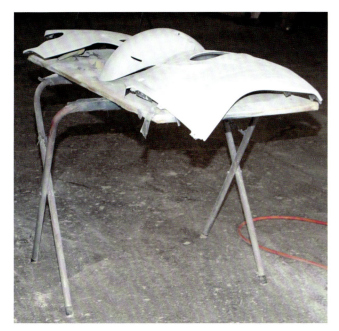

Folding stands hold work in progress

- **Pneumatic Sanders.** This type of sander is preferred for removing old paint from a part, smoothing the primer coats of paint and scuffing the surface of the base paint or clear coat in preparation of airbrushing.

The pneumatic sander is indispensable in a full-blown body shop

You will encounter parts that are better suited for hand sanding rather than using air tools, due to their shape or size, such as motorcycle tanks and fenders.

- **Electric Buffer.** Interchangeable pads attach to the buffer wheel to provide a soft, clean surface to polish the clear coat. There are buffer kits that contain specialized pads that work well on small or odd-shaped objects.

Interchangeable pads on the electric buffer polish the clear coat to a high luster

Accessories are the same as listed for the specialty paint shop.

- **Advantages.** You will have total control of the painting and finishing process, ensuring quality and timely completion. You make more money; the average invoice amount is much more for a complete paint job than for just custom graphics.

> **ASSORTED TIPS & WORDS OF WISDOM**
> *If the customer says "Money is no object," it will be. Guaranteed!*

> **ASSORTED TIPS & WORDS OF WISDOM**
> *Write everything down. All details should be discussed and agreed upon by the customer and yourself, and recorded.*

AUTO-SHOP REQUIREMENTS

CHAPTER TWO

Auto-Painting Accessories

These items are recommended for both full-service and specialty paint shops.

- **Masking Machine.** This tool holds various sizes of masking paper with masking tape affixed to one edge, and dispenses it, facilitating the process of masking out a vehicle or areas adjacent to where painting will occur.

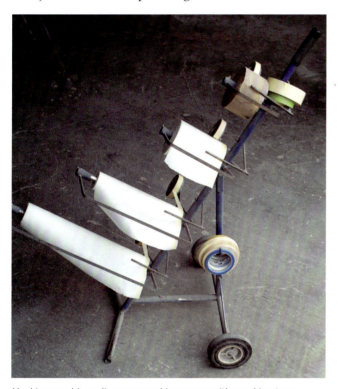

Masking machines dispense masking paper with masking tape affixed along one edge, speeding the masking process greatly.

- **Wet-Sanding Paper.** You should stock grades from semi-coarse (500 grit) to super-fine (3000 grit).

Grades of wet/dry sandpaper commonly used for custom painting include grits from 500 (coarse) – 1200 (very fine)

- **Scuff Pads.** These are also available in fine to coarse grades. They work well on edges and irregular surfaces.

Assorted Tips & Words of Wisdom

Keep your carbon air respirator in its plastic bag when not in use. The carbon in the filter saturates and is rendered inert by the time it is exposed in the shop environment. Exchange the cotton pre-filter on the outside of the mask to keep the carbon filter from clogging prematurely.

- **In-line Air Pressure Regulator.** Wherever you are painting, you can control your air pressure with this piece of equipment. Connect the regulator between the air line and the airbrush or air gun.

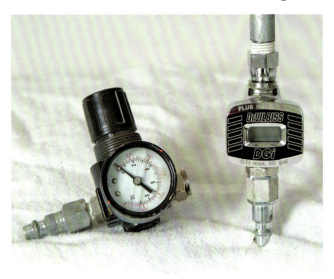

The regulator is connected via quick-disconnects between the air line and the air gun

- **Mixing Cups with Lids.** These translucent solvent-proof cups that have measuring scales embossed on their sides are very useful for mixing colors and saving non-catalyzed custom mixed colors. They are available in 8 oz. to 1 qt. cups. Wooden paint-mixing sticks are free where you buy your auto pants.

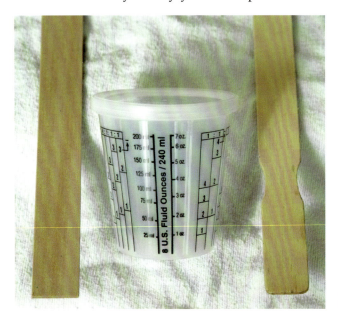

Stir sticks are free from most paint vendors. Measuring cups with lids aid in mixing the paint and additives at the correct ratios. The cups work well as custom-color storage containers.

- **Paint Shakers and Paint Filters.** A paint shaker agitates the paint to sufficiently distribute the pigments throughout its container. Stir sticks assist custom-color mixing and when testing paint viscosity. Paint filters should be used when transferring paints from the can into the paint gun or custom-color mixing cup. They are available at no cost where you purchase your paint. The free filters have a cotton element that works well to remove any unwanted particles from the paint but may add its own fibers to the mix. Higher-quality paint filters feature nylon elements that can be purchased at a nominal price. They will not shed any foreign matter into the paint and have dedicated styles for filtering either base coats or clear coats. The filter mesh for base coats is finer (190 microns) than that for clear-coat paint (150 microns).

Paint shakers thoroughly mix all paints before use

Assorted Tips & Words of Wisdom

Wear your respirator every time you mix, spray or clean with solvents. Your loved ones will appreciate having you around later.

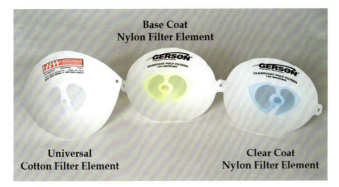

Specialized filters for specific applications

- **3M Masking Tapes.** Sizes range from 1/16 to 3 inches. I only use 3M tapes. The tack is perfect, so it leaves a minimal residue of its adhesive behind when it is removed from a painted surface. What little residue that is present is easily cleaned away with RM Pre-Kleeno 901. Thirty years of custom painting has taught me that 3M tapes perform to the highest standards.

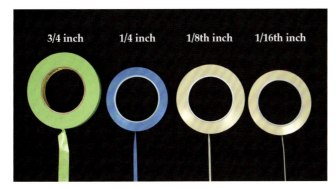

Essential tape widths to stock

- **Tack Rags.** These sticky cloths clean dust from a painted surface when lightly wiped over it, leaving no residue.

Sticky tack rags clean dust and other particulates from a painted surface prior to adding more paint

- **Airbrush-Paint Bottles.** These are necessary for siphon-feed airbrushes. Bottles of various sizes and shapes are available.

Paint bottles designed for use with siphon and side-feed airbrushes are offered in sizes of 1 ounce – 5 ounces. Choose the capacity to match the size of the assignment. I often seal these bottles and use them to store uncatalyzed custom-mixed colors for future use.

Assorted Tips & Words of Wisdom

Your tack rag should be kept in a clean plastic "baggie" after it is opened to keep foreign objects from sticking to it. Nothing is worse than wiping your fresh paint with shop grit.

- **Airbrush and Air Gun Cleaning Kits**. A metal butcher tray (available at art stores) is great when disassembling airbrushes and air guns in order to clean the parts.

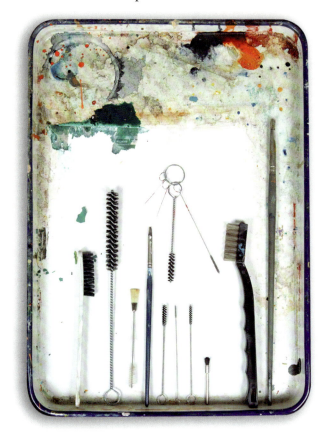

I use an assortment of brushes and solvents to clean all of my airbrushes and air guns. A butcher tray contains the airbrush-cleaning tools.

- **X-Acto Knives.** You should be sure to have plenty of extra replacement blades. I use the #11 blade size exclusively.

- **Artool Multi-Rail/Bridge**. It is used as a bridge to protect artwork from rubs and smears while painting.

X-Acto knives and Artool Multi-Rail.

- **Self-Healing Cutting Mat.** You will want these to cut your custom masks and stencils on. I use the largest size in my automotive shop. Smaller sizes are useful when working on smaller designs or when you must work away from your studio.

Self-healing cutting mats are used to cut stencils and shields on. They do not dull the blade, and they offer a smooth surface for accurate cutting

- **Drafting Film and Artists' Repositionable Adhesive**. I prefer drafting film that is matte on one side and glossy on the other to create custom stencils. Use a pencil to draw on the matte side, and cut or burn on the glossy. The X-Acto knife glides easily on the smooth surface, and the matte side has enough tooth to hold onto the pencil graphite. It is dimensionally stable, which means it won't stretch out of shape while handling. Because it is so stable, it is repositionable when used with the proper adhesive. I prefer 3M repositionable adhesive for its ability to hold the stencil in place while painting and because its residue is easily cleaned from the painted surface with RM 901.

Assorted Tips & Words of Wisdom

Never do sketches or layouts for free. Always get a deposit! The bigger the job the bigger the deposit needs to be.

Drafting film is available in sheets or rolls up to 48 inches

- **Stencil Burners.** These are used to cut the drafting film by actually melting it. A very fine burning tip is essential. A smooth sheet of glass, metal or tile surface to burn stencils on is also recommended. The cool surface will retard the melting process of the stencil material after the hot tip of the stencil burner is removed from it.

Electric or butane stencil burners are available. Burners are used to cut organic shapes in drafting film or stretch mask.

- **Hand-Held Shields.** Artool Products manufactures several commercially produced shields eliminating the need to mask around small objects during the course of painting. Their multi-faceted nature makes them a time and labor saver. Many unique and exciting shields also open up a world of creativity. Consider them an indispensable addition to your painting toolbox. Artool airbrush shields are available at most automotive jobber shops.

- **Airbrush Holders and Air Gun Holders.** These are a *must-have* item. Locate them around your workspace so you can set the airbrush or gun down safely and securely as the situation arises. Make sure to dedicate a couple of holders for your road kit.

Artists' spray mount from 3M is my choice for a repositionable adhesive

These holders offer a secure place to store an air gun or hold it in an upright position as paint is added to the cup

above: Artool shields; Lucky 13, Cloud Nine, Tiki Master, Inferno, FH-2, Devil or Angel, Flame-O-Rama Funkadelik, Super Shield, Nutz 'N Boltz and Flame-Dango. Learn about these and dozens more at ArtoolProducts.com

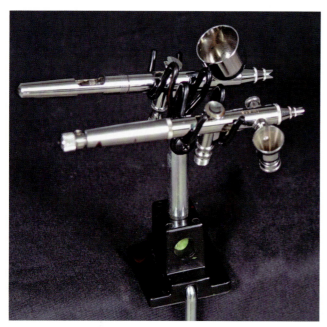

Airbrush holders are an essential accessory

- **Vinyl Plotter/Cutter**. This is quickly becoming a must-have item. It works in conjunction with a computer to cut a stencil out of a material that is generically referred to as paint mask. Once cut, the stencil is applied with a product called transfer tape. Transfer tape comes in widths that match standard vinyl roll sizes. The adhesive that covers one side of the transfer tape picks the computer-cut design from its backing paper and keeps it registered properly as it is moved from the plotter to the vehicle or part that you are painting. Properly positioning the stencil on the first try is imperative since once placed, it cannot be adjusted. Any alignment errors will require the misaligned stencil to be removed and a replacement cut by the plotter. Plotters are especially well suited to lettering and graphics. An internet search for vinyl plotters will return thousands of suppliers.

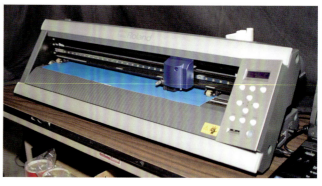

Vinyl plotters save time by custom cutting stencils out of Paint Mask with incredible accuracy

- **Projectors.** I use mine to transfer the art from my sketch paper or photo to the matte side of the drafting film. I project the image onto the film and trace the details with a lead pencil. Projectors are generally useful in design layout.

I use the projector to transfer my drawings onto the stencil material

- **Masking Paper.** You should stock widths from 6 to 48 inches. Vinyl transfer tape performs double duty as great masking paper, in addition to supporting the vinyl plotter/cutter operations.

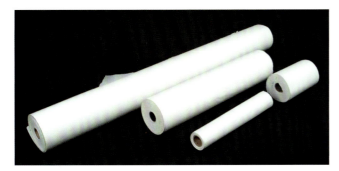

Masking papers are available in a plethora of sizes and colors. I prefer white, because I test my airbrush and check my color on it as I paint.

- **Plastic Sheeting.** This material can be used as an economical and practical means of protecting parts and other areas of the shop from dust created from sanding and paint over-spray.

- **Artool Ultra Mask.** This low-tack masking film for airbrushing graphics on anything is translucent, solvent-proof and repositionable. It also has a paper backing so you can run it through your plotter.

- **Hand Cleaners.** You will want cleaners specifically developed to remove automotive paint from your hands. Traditionally, this type of item is sold in a cream form in a jar. One of the new innovations that I prefer are fabric hand cleaners that are dispensed from a bucket and impregnated with paint removers and skin conditioners.

Hand cleaners come in tubes, tubs and sheets

ASSORTED TIPS & WORDS OF WISDOM

Never skimp on materials or your equipment. Your reputation depends on them.

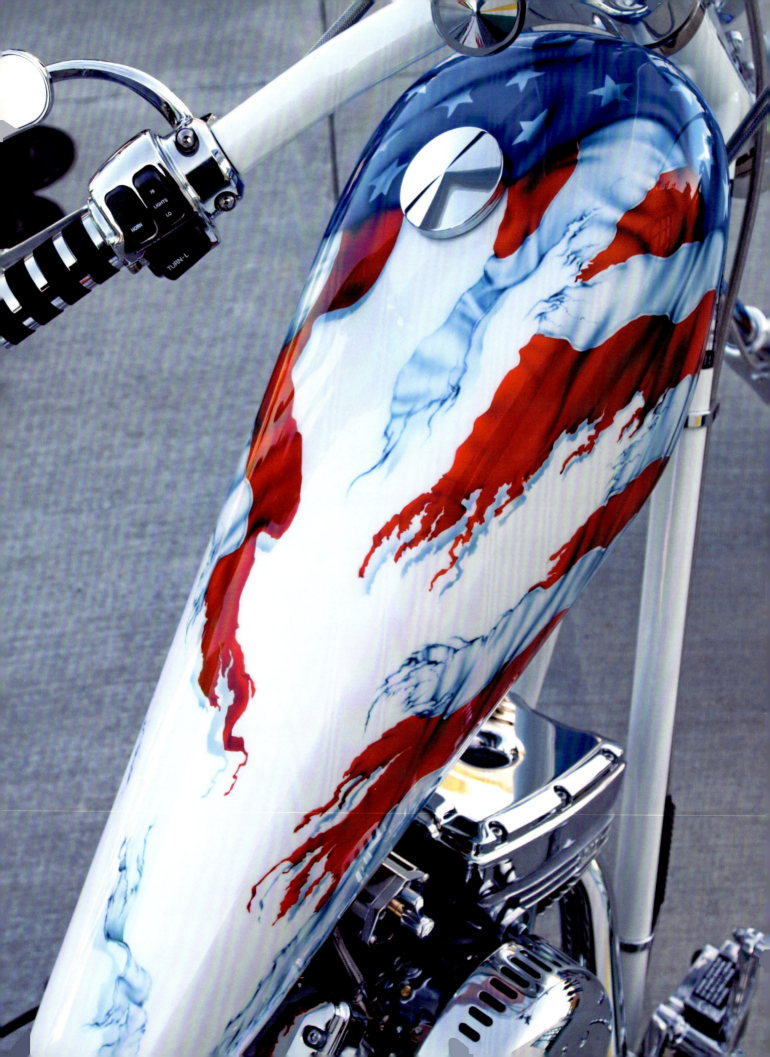

CHAPTER THREE

Paints & Additives

Most beginners find that gaining an understanding of automotive paints is probably one of the most confusing parts of establishing a custom-painting business. The amount of data that needs to be digested can be overwhelming for a novice. Let's cut through all of the data and give you the information that you need to get started painting on a small scale.

Major paint brands (manufacturers) offer various types, or "lines," of paint. Every paint line has a unique chemistry that affects how it sands, sprays, dries and interacts with the other chemical products used during the painting process.

As a general rule, it is unwise to mix the paints and additives of different paint lines with one another. It will void any warranty that the manufacturer offers and most probably will affect the performance of the paint. With that said, there are reducers and clear coats that are chemically compatible with other paint lines within their brand. A custom painter learns these nuances with experience, but a novice should not take chances. Only use the reducers and additives recommended on your paint container.

You should be familiar with paint systems from several major paint manufacturers, since your customer vehicles will most likely be coated with one of them. Major automotive-paint brands include R+M, Glasurit, Sikkens, DuPont, House of Kolor, Valspar, PPG, SEM and Auto Air.

For the airbrush painter, I would recommend stocking only one paint line of whichever paint brand you wish to use. That's because airbrushed art and lettering dries so quickly, it does not chemically interact with the base paint or clear coat it is sprayed over as it would if applied with a large spray gun. This characteristic lets you use your airbrush to spray your brand of paint over any other brand with negligible ill effect. The part or vehicle can be clear coated after the airbrushing is complete, and the clear coat bonds to its compatible base coat as if the airbrushing wasn't even there.

Keeping up with paint chemistry and technology is akin to staying up-to-date with medical or computer advances. You need to keep learning every day or you fall behind.

Do not be afraid to consult with the paint and materials specialists that work at the local automotive-paint supply where you are buying your paint and accessories. They will have the most up-to-date information on the latest products.

No matter which brand or type of paint you are using, you must follow the instructions for that specific brand of paint. When the paint is purchased, request the tech sheet from the vendor that informs you about the mixing ratios, application rates, temperature requirements and other variables that the must be observed. Be aware that the instructions refer to painting with large spray guns. Mixing paint for the airbrush allows for some liberties to be taken with the mixing ratio of reducers; otherwise, follow the paint manufacturers mixing instructions for any of the other additives.

The instructions on the "Tech Sheet" or "Product Information Sheet" includes information that specifies the percentage of paint to reducer and hardener (if applicable). Some paints come ready to spray and require no additives. Always read the instructions on the paint can or the paint tech sheet to ascertain the correct mixing ratios and additives for the type of paint you are using. You will also want a Material Safety Dara Sheet (MSDS) that describes the hazardous materials in the paint and additives.

Application recommendations Tech sheets inform you about:
- The number of paint coats required to attain complete coverage
- How many square feet a gallon of paint will cover if the paint must be baked to cure
- How much air pressure to use when spraying the paint
- The correct shop temperature for the paint to cure properly
- The estimated paint-drying time

Sanding and polishing recommendations which inform you which grit sandpapers and polishing compounds to use during the painting process.

Choices for Automotive Paints and Additives:

Paint reducers are used to thin down the paint for spraying. They are available in slow, medium and fast flash rates. The flash rate indicates how fast the reducer evaporates out of the paint. In cold, wet weather you need a fast reducer so the paint will dry within the recommended time window. Hot, humid conditions cause the solvents in the paint to evaporate very quickly, so a slower reducer is needed to offset the effect. A medium-speed reducer works 90% of the time for me, because the over-reduced paints that I spray are applied very lightly and dry on contact with the surface. Much more attention needs to be paid to reducer speed when painting base coats and clear coats, because the paint stays wet much longer after it hits the surface.

Matching a reducer speed to the ambient conditions can be accomplished by employing the "Law of Ten." This benchmark for automotive painting states that all paints are best sprayed at 75 degrees Fahrenheit.

If the temperature increases to 85 degrees, the same paint will dry twice as fast. This situation would require a slow reducer to retard the drying process.

If the paint is sprayed at 65 degrees, it will take twice as long to dry. This situation calls for a fast reducer to speed the dry time.

Hardeners/catalysts are chemical agents that when mixed into the paint at appropriate ratios, cause it to harden within a predictable time frame.

> **ASSORTED TIPS & WORDS OF WISDOM**
>
> *Paints that do not require a catalyst can be mixed and saved on the shelf for months. Custom colors like flesh tones can be saved for later assignments, saving you money.*

Lacquer paint and custom painting have traditionally walked hand in hand. The color choices available have always been awesome, as well as the candy, pearl and metallic paint effects lacquers offer. The fast cure/dry time for the paint is perfect for painting stripes and other custom appointments. It can be taped over shortly after spraying and not pull up when the tape is removed. Lacquer paint sands easy and layers/blends well, which makes it easy to repair. Lacquer reducer is added to the paint at a various ratios, depending on paint brand to thin it for spraying purposes. When airbrushing I reduce the paint by a 2-to-1 ratio (two parts reducer to one part paint), up to as much as 3-to-1. The airbrushed paint dries immediately upon contact with the surface. Depending on the ambient conditions, it only takes a few minutes before airbrushed lacquer can be masked over or taped on with no adverse consequences.

Lacquer-based paint requires clear coat paint to be applied over it. Lacquer clear coat can be built up many layers, then sanded and polished to an ultra-high-gloss finish.

Urethane clear coats can normally be sprayed over lacquer base coats to protect them with no ill effect. Urethane clear is much harder and more chip-resistant than lacquer clear coat. Note that lacquer clear coat should never be sprayed over enamel or urethane-based paints.

Environmental reforms will eventually eliminate lacquer paints from everyday use. They are still available at the time of this writing, but they are going the way of the dinosaur. I do not recommend investing in this type of paint.

Automotive enamel paint was originally a "one-stage" paint that required no clear coat. It was used to paint the first Ford automobiles back in the 1930s and '40s in Detroit Michigan.

Eventually two-stage enamels were introduced. The second stage (clear coat) offered a higher luster and better paint protection. Some enamel paints require a catalyst to be added to make it harden. Once the catalyst is added, the paint must be sprayed within a certain time before it begins to harden in the spray gun or mixing cup. The best

qualities of enamel paints are durability and ease of application. Single-stage and two-stage enamel paints are commonly used in auto repair and new equipment production.

Urethane-based paints spray easy, dry fast and have a chip-resistant shine. I estimate that 90% of today's automotive paints are either acrylic- or polyester-based. Urethane-based paints offer a myriad of color and special-effect choices. Urethane paints can be single-stage or two-stage. Some require a catalyst to harden, while others do not.

I prefer to paint with uncatalyzed paints, so I need not worry about working times and I can save my leftover paint for future use in a sealed plastic mixing cup. Urethane-based paint requires a urethane clear coat. Lacquer clear coat will not adhere properly to a urethane base coat.

Polyester paints are composed of dyes or other concentrated pigments suspended in polyester resins. The dyes are transparent and could be equated to a candy color. They can be reduced or sprayed right out of the can at full strength. A hardener can be added to the paint to inhibit color bleed between layers. The opaque color pigments offer excellent color choices and flow smoothly through the airbrush or air gun. Urethane clear coat is recommended for these paints.

Waterborne paints are evolving on a daily basis. Progressive environmental laws will eventually outlaw solvent-based paints. Lacquer, enamel and urethane paints most likely will be unavailable in the future. The color and spraying qualities of water-based paints are getting better ever day. In my opinion, they still have a long way to go to match the performance of urethanes and polyester dyes. Most waterborne paints require bonding agents, thinning mediums and longer drying times than solvent-based paints, which makes them a little harder to work with and less time-efficient. A paint-dryer (heat) gun is often employed to accelerate drying times. This type of paint is the future, so it makes sense to get acquainted with its properties.

Volatile organic compounds (VOCs), hazardous air-polluting solvents (HAPS) and isocyanides are present in most solvent-based paints. Use proper safety measures to protect your eyes, skin and respiration.

Assorted Tips & Words of Wisdom

If you are like me and prefer to use paints that do not require activators or catalysts, you can mix all the colors that you expect to use before you begin painting. This makes it easy to get into the flow when you are painting.

CHAPTER FOUR

Airbrush / Air Gun Choices

Every airbrush artist should be prepared to paint at whatever scale the client requires. That means stocking air guns and airbrushes that are capable of painting large areas and very small details.

Ensure that your compressor produces enough compressed air to keep up with the cfm (cubic feet per minute) rating of your airbrush or air guns. The cfm that air guns require can range from 1.0 to 20.0. Your air gun choices will determine how large your compressor will need to be.

Air gun operating air pressure is dictated by the specific paint gun model you choose and the viscosity of the paint you are using.

Depending on their intended application, air guns have paint nozzles measuring between .4 mm and 2.5 mm. These nozzle sizes will produce spray patterns from 1/8 to 15.7 inches. Spray patterns will be round or oval, depending on the design of the specific air gun.

Airbrushes feature paint-nozzle sizes ranging from .18 mm to .6 mm. They will produce spray patterns from a hair line to 2 inches wide. Normal operating air pressures range from 15 psi (pounds per square inch) to 60 psi, depending on the paint or the desired effect.

The many varieties of air guns and airbrushes that are available can make deciding which ones to buy difficult. Every brand has its unique features and recommended applications. Select the types and styles that fit your needs the best.

Professional painters should own quality equipment. My personal experience has taught me that there is a big difference between airbrush brands in terms of quality and customer service. I have found that Anest Iwata air guns and Iwata airbrushes are built to the highest standards. Their consistent quality makes them a solid investment and ensures that I have equipment that I can count on.

HVLP (high volume-low pressure)
Air Guns. These are available in gravity, side-feed or siphon-feed models. They are designed to spray at a lower air pressure than conventional spray guns. Low air consumption and superior atomization is the trademark of all HVLP air guns. These air guns feature "high–transfer efficiency," which means that approximately 80% of the sprayed paint adheres to the surface, resulting in minimal over-spray and less material waste.

Gravity-Feed Air Guns and Airbrushes. This is the most efficient painting system in terms of mechanical simplicity and ease of cleaning. Paint flows downward to the paint nozzle from the paint cup that is mounted immediately above it. There are no restrictions in the paint path, and the paint needs only to travel fractions of an inch to spray. This design makes the air gun very responsive to operator input. No other air gun style offers the level of detail and control that the gravity-feed airbrushes do.

Anest Iwata LPH400 LV offers low-air consumption

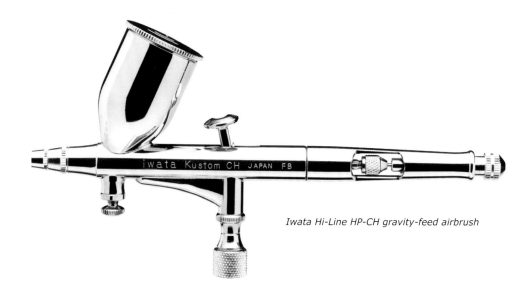

Iwata Hi-Line HP-CH gravity-feed airbrush

Side-Feed Air Guns and Airbrushes. These allow for painting 360 degrees because the color cup will rotate and lock in any position. This comes in handy when painting overhead or at odd angles. The side-mounted color cup also enables the painter to see the paint coming out of the gun better when painting very close to the surface. Since paint is gravity-fed, it naturally flows to the paint nozzle. The slightly longer paint path makes this style airbrush/air gun second only to the gravity-feed versions when it comes to mechanical efficiency.

The Iwata Kustom TH gravity-feed airbrush features both fan and round pattern spray nozzles, and comes complete with a MAC Valve (Micro Air Control)

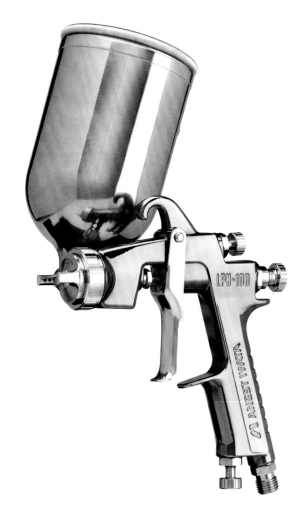

Anest Iwata LPH100 LVG side-feed air gun

Iwata Kustom Micron CM airbrush

Siphon-Feed Air Guns and Airbrushes. These models draw their paints via a tube from a cup that is attached below the paint nozzle. Compressed air combines with the paint in the head assembly of the air gun. This type of gun is the least efficient in terms of mechanics and responsiveness, since the paint has a greater distance to travel before atomization. Some painters love their large siphon-feed air guns. I can appreciate the balance of the paint cup against the air line, with the hand as the fulcrum.

Siphon-feed airbrushes do have advantages. I use a siphon-feed airbrush 90% of the time (see Iwata HP BC below). Color bottles of various sizes attach to the airbrush. I can mix paint in a variety of colors in advance and interchange them as I paint. This system of color changing is very efficient for automotive airbrushing.

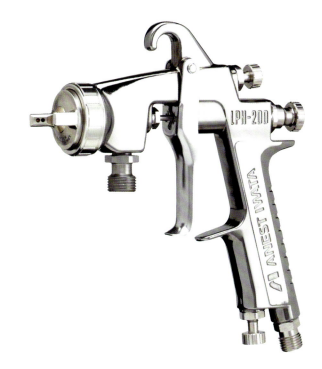

Anest Iwata LPH200 LVP siphon-feed air gun

Regardless of type, airbrushes with paint nozzles of .18 mm to .35 mm are considered detail-oriented (see Iwata Kustom Micron CM above). Use them to color small areas or create tiny detail. Airbrushes with paint nozzles from .35 mm to .6 mm are best suited to airbrush larger areas or to spray more viscous paints.

Larger air guns with paint nozzles of .4 mm to 1.0 mm are considered detail or specialty air guns. They produce spray widths of 1/8th to 4 inches. I use these models to paint art freehand on areas that are too big for a standard airbrush. They also work well for spraying backgrounds or parts that are not too large.

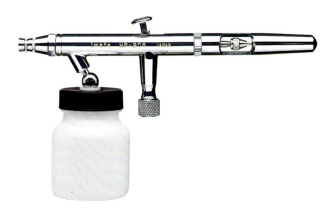

Iwata HP BC Plus siphon-feed airbrush

Guns with paint-nozzle sizes greater than 1.0 mm are more for standard painting applications, like spraying primers, base coats and clear coats. Most standard guns spray patterns of 4 to 15 inches.

CHAPTER FIVE

Airbrush / Air Gun Operation

The first step to becoming an expert custom painter is to understand the correct way to operate your airbrush or air gun. There are two types of airbrushes available, single-action and double-action.

Professional air guns have a two-stage paint/air trigger. They relate directly to the dual action airbrushes in their method of operation. These "methods" are like learning to ride a bicycle. After they are mastered, the process becomes almost automatic.

A single-action airbrush will work fine for painting that does not require much variation. They work best where the exact same spray width is needed for every job. Single-action airbrushes operate like a can of spray paint: one action (pressing down on the trigger) delivers both air and paint. While single-actions offer you control over air pressure and paint flow, they have inherent drawbacks that make them less than desirable for rendering complex artwork. The most notable drawback is that they will not spray air only.

The dual-action airbrush offers the most responsive control of the spray pattern possible and lets you make intuitive adjustments as you paint. This makes it much more efficient to use from an artist's viewpoint. In my opinion, dual-action airbrushes are an absolute necessity when painting any art or lettering freehand. All of the examples in this book demonstrate dual-action airbrush techniques.

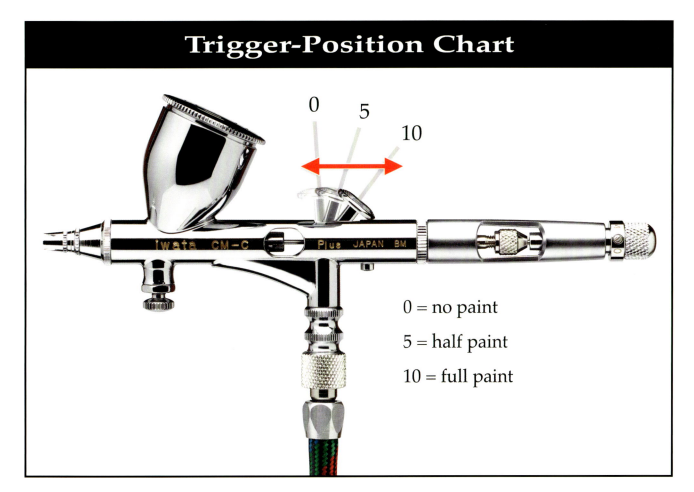

> **ASSORTED TIPS & WORDS OF WISDOM**
>
> *Store your airbrushes with a very light coat of petroleum jelly on the paint needle to ensure like-new performance the next time it is used. Make sure to clean the needle before airbrushing.*

The following describes the operation of dual-action airbrushes and two-stage air guns. Dual-action refers to the two trigger motions that must be executed to make the airbrush spray pigments.

- The first action is to push the paint trigger down as far as it will go to spray air only.

- Once the air is flowing, continue to hold the trigger down and rock it backwards (action 2) to initiate paint flow. As the trigger is rocked further backwards, more paint will be mixed into the airflow.

- Allowing the trigger to move forward terminates paint flow.

- Rocking the trigger to and fro slides the paint needle in and out of the paint nozzle that is in the head of the airbrush. As the needle is backed away from the paint nozzle, it leaves more room for paint to pass through the nozzle's orifice.

- Always remember to keep the airbrush trigger depressed to keep clean air flowing through your airbrush between paint strokes. The constant airflow keeps paint from building up on the airbrush's or air gun's paint needle. This is an important point to note, because excess paint that has built up on the needle's tip will spit the next time airflow is initiated.

- Keep in mind that as the airbrush moves closer to the surface to paint smaller details, you must reduce the volume of paint exiting the airbrush to avoid paint runs and sags.

Airbrush Operation Demonstration.

All airbrushed art and lettering is built on three basic building blocks: the dot, the line and the gradation. No matter what the image is, it can be broken down into these three basic operations. Dots should appear round. Lines should have tapered ends. A gradation is when the color fades from dark to light evenly.

Before painting on anything, it is best to understand how to hold the airbrush and what happens when it is operated.

- Attach a paint bottle filled with paint, or add paint to the color cup.

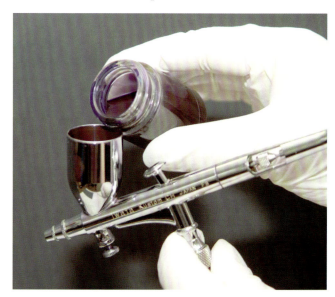

Add paint to the airbrush

> **ASSORTED TIPS & WORDS OF WISDOM**
>
> *Airbrush hand cramp is caused by a number of factors. Because airbrushing requires many thousands of minute finger movements, fatigue does play a part in cramping. Try to hold the airbrush with your fingers extended. Your hand should not be fist-like when holding the airbrush. An open-handed approach will let your finger joints work together to gain the control you desire. The most important thing to remember is that everyone has different hand and finger sizes so the grip is different for every person.*

- Hold the airbrush between your thumb and middle finger. Place the tip of your index finger on the paint lever (trigger). Everyone's hand is different: find a grip that is comfortable for you based on this model.

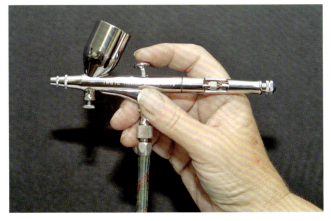

Airbrush grip

- Press the trigger down all the way to initiate clean air flow.

Press the trigger down completely

- Ease the trigger backward slowly. Imagine 10 trigger positions with 0 being no material spraying and 10 equaling the maximum amount of material the airbrush will spray. Spray the paint into the air away from your face. Take care to maintain the same distance across the entire surface. Observe the amount of paint exiting the airbrush at the various trigger positions.

ASSORTED TIPS & WORDS OF WISDOM

No joke!!! Open flames and shop fumes mix.... and combust. No smoking around your supplies.

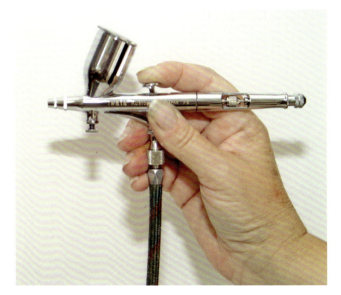

Rocking the trigger backwards

Also notice the shape of the spray pattern. It is very small at the tip of the airbrush and gets wider the further it sprays from the airbrush.

Cone-shaped airbrush spray

- Push the trigger forward to cease spraying.

Rock the trigger forward to cease spraying

The only other consideration to take into account when operating the airbrush or air gun is the distance to the surface that it is held when sprayed. Because the paint exits the airbrush in the shape of a cone, the spray pattern is very thin at the airbrush's or air gun's paint nozzle and gets increasingly wider the farther it sprays. Therefore, creating tight, minute details requires working close to the surface, and rendering soft details or color-blending is best accomplished by spraying from a greater distance.

Every airbrush pass should start with the trigger pushed down and in the 0 position. It will be rocked backward to the appropriate 0-10 position for the situation and returned to the 0 position to curtail paint flow.

Now that I've explained how to operate the airbrush, it is time to create the three basic building blocks of airbrushing.

Creating a Dot.

- Attach a paint bottle or fill the paint cup. Test the airbrush by pressing the trigger down for clean air. If it produces clean air with no paint mixed in, you are ready to paint. If paint is mixing in with no backward movement of the trigger, the needle is not properly seated in the airbrush and is allowing paint to pass through the paint nozzle. Check the needle and reset its position, and start the test again.

Once the airbrush is working properly:

- Point the airbrush at the surface from a distance of approximately 2 inches.

Hold the airbrush 2 inches from the surface

- Depress the trigger straight down to spray clean air only.

- Ease the trigger backward to approximately position 3 and hold it there; notice that the paint is building into a dot.

ASSORTED TIPS & WORDS OF WISDOM

Every airbrush paint stroke or "pass" should consist of 1 pull and 1 push action on the operator's part. Failure to do so will cause the pigment to build up on the paint needle. As the paint builds on the tip, it causes the spray pattern to widen and eventually the paint to spit.

Paint builds to a dot

- Before the dot becomes a drip or sag, push the trigger forward to curtail paint application. Keep the trigger depressed to keep the air spraying during the entire operation.

Rock trigger forward to cease paint flow

You should have a soft-edged dot with no paint spider webs or paint sags. If sags do appear, too much paint was applied.

Assorted Tips & Words of Wisdom
I cannot emphasize enough how important it is to keep your airbrush clean. If it has any foreign material dried in it, the airbrush will not perform properly.

Creating a Line (Dagger Stroke).

A proper line created by an airbrush has pointed ends. These pointed ends and the thicker line that connect them resemble the shape of a dagger, thus the name "dagger stroke."

When you can paint dagger lines consistently it indicates that you have mastered your trigger control enough to render most airbrush effects.

- Attach a paint bottle or fill the paint cup. Test the airbrush by the aforementioned method.

Once you are sure that your airbrush is working properly:

- Point the airbrush at the surface at a distance of 1/2 inch.

- Depress the trigger to spray clean air only.

- Start moving the airbrush horizontally at a slow speed and ease the trigger backwards as you move the airbrush until you notice the paint making a line across the surface.

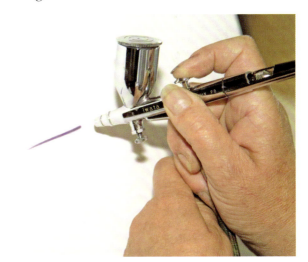
Easing the trigger backwards

- Once the airbrushed line is apparent, discontinue the backward movement of the trigger and hold the trigger steady in that position to continue the line.

Painting the line

Too faint a line could mean that you need more paint. Splattering or dripping indicates that you pulled the trigger back too far and applied too much paint. How far back you pull the lever depends on the nozzle size of your airbrush, paint viscosity and distance to the surface.

- To end the line, ease the trigger forward while continuing to move the airbrush along the imaginary line until the paint line tapers off to a nice point.

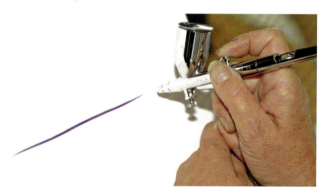

Push forward to cease painting

- Repeat the line in the opposite direction.

- Every line should begin and end with a nice tapering point. When it does, it resembles the dagger shape. Dagger strokes can be fat, skinny or anywhere in between, depending on how you move the airbrush and manipulate the trigger.

- If the airbrush is held closer to the surface, the dot or line will be smaller - hold the airbrush farther away, and the lines or dots will be larger and thicker.

Practice painting dots and lines of every size and thickness until you can do them with control and confidence.

Painting a Gradation.

Gradations are used in many ways. The most common is to color a specific area within a cut stencil or to freehand paint a background.

- Attach a paint bottle or fill your paint cup. Test the airbrush by using the aforementioned method.

Once the airbrush is working properly:

- Hold the airbrush 8 - 10 inches from the surface.

Airbrush is 8 to 10 inches from the surface

- Slowly move the airbrush in a horizontal line from left to right and ease the airbrush's trigger back to the 8 or 9 position. Hold it there as you continue to move the airbrush along its path.

Trigger rocked back to the 8-9 position

ASSORTED TIPS & WORDS OF WISDOM

Never use cotton swabs to clean an airbrush. The cotton filaments can remain behind in the airbrush and cause a blockage once it gets into the paint nozzle.

- Ease the trigger forward to the 0 position as the spray pattern approaches the right edge. Keep moving the airbrush. The paint should be tapered to 0 before reaching the edge of the test area, but the air should be kept on. Do not release the air at the end of the pass. Take care to maintain the same distance to the surface across the entire area.

- Repeat the process from right to left. Overlap the first pass by one-half.

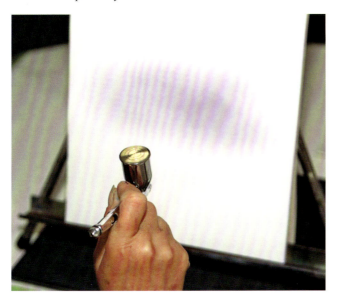

Repeat process right to left

- Repeat the process from left to right. Overlap the previous pass by one-half.

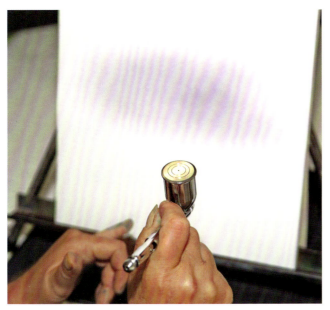

Repeat process left to right

- Continue to the bottom of the test area by painting back and forth across the surface and overlapping each pass by one-half.

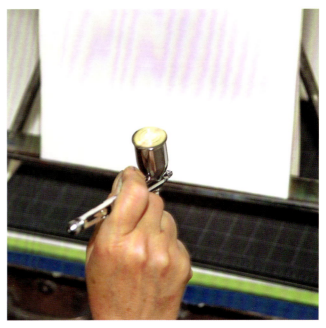

Overlap paint passes by one-half

At this point, there should be a light coat of paint from top to bottom

Your finished exercise should display a gradual fade (gradation) from the darker central area to the lighter edges.

Gradual paint fade from dark to light

If you do not have banding (obvious lines), dark blotches or light spots in the paint, congratulations!

You have mastered the gradation. You are now armed with the three building blocks of airbrush painting.

I advise painting dots, lines and gradations on paper with water-based airbrush paint to begin with and moving on to non-porous automotive surfaces and automotive paints once you are comfortable working on the more forgiving porous surfaces.

Air Gun Operation.

Automotive spray guns feature a two-stage paint lever (trigger) that equates to the double action airbrush. When the lever is squeezed to the first stop, the only thing that comes out of the gun is clean air.

Squeeze trigger until you feel the first stop

ASSORTED TIPS & WORDS OF WISDOM

Adjust your airbrushing "Angle of Attack" by raising or lowering the object that you are painting so your wrist is in a comfortable position in relation to the airbrush. This will facilitate better trigger control and alleviate hand and wrist fatigue.

Squeezing more takes the trigger past the first stop into the second stage. The second stage pulls the needle away from the paint nozzle causing the paint to mix with air to create the spray pattern.

Squeeze trigger to the second stop

There are control knobs on the backside of the air gun. One will control the air flow through the air gun and adjusts the spray pattern when it is turned.

Adjusting the spray pattern

The second control knob limits the paint needle's travel. It can be pre-set to stop at just the perfect paint flow for your application when the trigger is squeezed to the limit of the second stage.

Setting the limit of the paint-needle travel

Assorted Tips & Words of Wisdom

Stocking your provisions with spare airbrushes is essential, especially when you are working in someone else's shop. One unfortunate drop can end the day if you are not prepared.

Air Gun Painting Exercise.

Even though I prefer not to offer complete paint service, I still need to understand the process. Because airbrushing is sandwiched between the color (base) coat of paint and the final clear coat, if any part of the paint work is poorly done, it affects the quality of the entire paint job, including the airbrushing.

Here is a list that explains the purpose of each part of a paint job.

Primer Paint. Primer is sprayed with a large spray gun over bare aluminum that has been smoothed and cleaned in preparation for painting. Once primer is sprayed, it seals the metal and any body filler that might have been applied.

Primer is sprayed

The primer is sanded with 500-grit sandpaper to give it some tooth for the base color to stick to.

Primer is sanded

After sanding, an ultra fine scuff-pad is used to touch up the edges where sandpaper would burn through the paint. Next, the primed surface is cleaned with a fast evaporating degreaser.

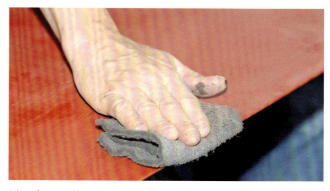
Ultra-fine scuff pad

Apply the cleaner (RM 901) with a clean soft cotton cloth. Dry the surface with a soft cotton cloth as soon as possible after cleaning. A good technique is to have the wet cloth in one hand and the dry cloth in the other. Do not let the cleaner evaporate on its own, or it will leave rings on the paint that are difficult to remove without sanding.

RM 901 Pre-Kleeno removes contaminants

Assorted Tips & Words of Wisdom

Use the fastest evaporating pre-cleaner possible. Any metal or paint cleaners that remain wet for too long on the surface can cause the airbrushed paint to start moving and blur the artwork.

Before clear coat is sprayed, clean off any incidental dust with a tack rag.

Tack rag cleans dust

Base Coat/Color Coat. This is the paint that contains the color that the parts or vehicle will be after painting. Multiple coats are required to get even coverage.

Clear Coat. After the color/base coat has dried, clear coat is sprayed to protect the color coat. If airbrushing is required, the clear coat, once dried, is wet-sanded with 800-grit sandpaper. The airbrushing is applied and then clear coated over to protect the airbrushing. After the final clear coat dries, it can be polished to a high luster.

Painting an evenly colored and adequately covered test panel is usually the goal when using a spray gun to apply primer paints, base paints and clear coats. The goal is to get the maximum effect from the least amount of paint. To do this, mix and apply the paint according to the manufacturer's instructions, and apply the paint using the overlapping methods described.

Knowing when to stop spraying the paint is also an important consideration. Over-application can be a big problem, so remember to take your time and observe what the paint is doing.

Air Gun Set-up.

For the purposes of testing, water can be sprayed with the air gun to understand how to adjust the controls on the air gun to modify the spray pattern and control the amount of material that is sprayed.

The following example will use RM Diamont automotive paint.

Paint shaker

- Add paint to the mixing cup.

Pour paint into mixing cup

AIRBRUSH / AIR GUN OPERATION   45

- Add reducer at the recommended ratio.

Add reducer

- Add the reduced paint to the air gun's color cup (be sure to use a paint-strainer).

Pour paint into air gun color cup

- Connect the air line from the compressor to the air gun. Refer to the air gun's packaging and the paint's tech sheet to determine the air pressure (pounds per square inch) at which the air gun and paint are designed to work best. Set the air pressure to the appropriate setting with the air pressure regulator on your compressor system.

- Point the air gun in a safe direction, and squeeze the paint lever/trigger until you feel resistance. The resistance is the limit of the first stage of trigger travel. Clean air will begin to escape the air gun through the air openings in the air gun's head assembly as soon as you start pulling the lever.

  Squeezing a bit more takes the lever past the first stage's limit and enters into the second stage. As soon as the second stage is initiated, the paint needle begins to back away from the paint nozzle. As the lever is squeezed backwards, the paint needle is pulled backwards with it. As the needle backs away from the paint nozzle, the material that you want to spray can pass through the orifice that the needle was blocking.

- Adjusting the airflow control on the back of the air gun while spraying will demonstrate the range of adjustment to the spray pattern that your air gun will provide to you. Common spray patterns are fan, round, tulip (C) and oval.

- Adjust the pre-set needle stop on the back of the air gun to limit how far the paint lever/trigger can be pulled away from the paint nozzle during the second stage of the lever pull. Set this control to deliver the optimal volume of paint/material desired when the lever is squeezed to the limit of the second stage.

- Keep in mind that there can be differences in the location of an air gun's control knobs, depending on manufacturer or model.

Painting a Test Panel.

- Make sure the air gun is clean, and mix up enough paint to color the test panel. Put the paint in the color cup. For this example, we will spray a color coat over an aluminum panel that has been primed with the appropriate primer paint.

- Make sure that the air pressure is set to match the specifications of your air gun.

- Before spraying the panel, check and adjust the spray pattern so it covers the panel efficiently. The spray pattern should be a long ellipse that evenly covers everything within its scope with paint.

- Clean the surface one more time with a tack rag to eliminate any dust.

- Hold the air gun 8 to 10 inches from the surface. Start off to the side of the panel. Squeeze the paint lever past the first stage to the limit of the second stage. Paint will be spraying. Make the first paint pass left to right across the top of the test panel. Don't be afraid to let a little bit of spray go over the edge ensuring edge-to-edge coverage.

- Once the right edge is reached, relax your grip on the paint lever allowing the return spring to position it to the first stage. Clean air is exiting the airbrush. Do not let the lever return to the off position.

- Initiate the next paint pass by squeezing the lever to the limit of the second stage and painting right to left. Overlap the first pass by one half. Remember to maintain the same distance from the surface on every pass.

Overlap by one-half. Maintain distance to surface

- Once the pass in completed, ease off of the lever to return it to the first stage.

ASSORTED TIPS & WORDS OF WISDOM

Always wet sand in the same direction when prepping any continuous surface like a car hood or cycle tank and fenders for a smoother look when completed.

ASSORTED TIPS & WORDS OF WISDOM

The higher the air pressure, the finer the dots will be in the airbrushed paint pattern. Conversely, low air pressure results in a spray pattern with larger dots of paint. Understanding these principles will aid in special-effect painting.

Repeat this process until you have completed the first coat. The first coat will not cover the primer paint completely. The primer will still be very apparent. Just be sure to keep the coverage even over the entire area.

First coat does not completely cover the primer

- Wait for the paint from the first coat to dry, and apply a second coat. Use the same overlapping method until adequate coverage has been attained. Always spray even coats from top to bottom, or the final paint may be flawed due to uneven coverage.

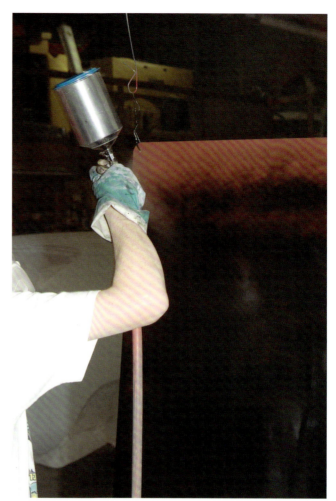

Strive for even coverage with good painting technique

- Once the color coat has dried, it can be clear coated in the same manner as it was colored.

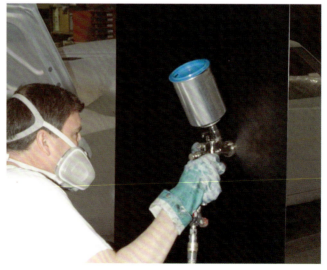

Color coat completed

- Mix enough clear coat for 2-3 coats in a mixing cup. Set your spray-gun controls to create the spray pattern you desire. Build the clear coat in the same manner as the color coat.

Mix the clear coat and hardener

- Spray even coats across the entire surface. Wait for each coat to dry before applying another. Once the clear coat has dried, for the prescribed amount of time as stated in its tech sheet, it can be buffed to a high sheen. If imperfections exist in the finish, they can be lightly wet-sanded away with 1000-1200 grit wet/dry sanding paper and then polished.

Clear coat ready for wet sanding

- If you are going to airbrush over the clear coat, wet-sand it with 800-grit paper to give the surface some tooth.

Dry-sanding with 800 grit

- The panel is now wet-sanded with 800-grit paper and ready for airbrushing.

Now sanded and ready for airbrush

Assorted Tips & Words of Wisdom

Pre-soak wet-sanding paper in clean water for at least 20 minutes to soften it. This helps prevent irregular deep scratches from occurring during the sanding process.

CHAPTER SIX

Masking Methods

Masking and stenciling are essentially the art of guarding against paint over-spray and under-spray. Masking protects from over-spray, while stenciling creates shapes by either eliminating or manipulating the paint sprayed along its borders.

Over-spray is paint that has been sprayed but did not come to rest in the target area. It floats about the shop, driven by the air currents in the workspace. Eventually, it finds its way onto any exposed surface in the form of paint dust. When painting with large spray guns, over-spray can be dramatically reduced by using a HVLP (high volume - low pressure) model. With this type of air gun, 80% of the paint sticks to the surface.

Under-spray is paint that encroaches under the tape or stencil edge that borders the painted design. Common causes for under-spray include:

- inadequate adhesive on the stencil material.

- stretching the masking tape too much while attempting to render the desired shape, which causes it to pull from the surface as it recoils back to its original tensile state.

- improper airbrush control. Concentrating the direction of the air-spray against the edges of stencils and shields can greatly increase under-spray.

The following are common items used for masking and stenciling. Choosing the best one for the application at hand makes the job more profitable by saving time and effort.

- **Masking Paper.** This product is commonly attached to the painting surface with 3/4" masking tape to protect against over-spray beyond the bounds of the stencil. Automotive masking papers are coated to make them paint-resistant and are commonly available in widths of 6" to 48".

- **Plastic Sheeting.** This material is used to protect large areas that lie beyond the masking paper's reach. It can be employed on the vehicle that is being painted or to protect objects or areas in the immediate vicinity of the vehicle when painting.

Plastic sheeting protects from dust and overspray

- **Transfer Tape.** It can be used as a masking agent, or it can be cut to fashion a stencil. Since it has an adhesive backing, it can be applied to the painting surface without tape. Once in place, a design can be drawn onto it and then carefully cut with an X-Acto knife. Once the cut design is removed, the transfer tape that is left on the vehicle creates the stencil.

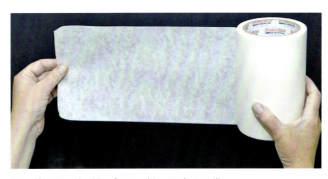

Transfer tape doubles for masking and stenciling

- **Drafting Film.** This is my number-1 choice for stenciling. It is solvent-proof and very translucent. I recommend using film with a slick, glossy finish on one side and a matte finish on the other. The matte side has enough tooth to hold graphite drawings, and the X-Acto knife glides smoothly when it is used on the glossy side. Using the X-Acto knife on the glossy side has the additional benefit of not smudging the graphite during the cutting process.

Drafting film on 100-foot roll

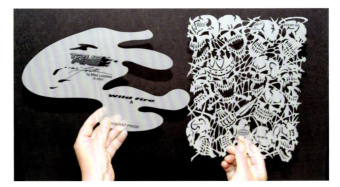

Hand-held shields save time and create details easily

Drafting film is dimensionally stable, which means that it will not stretch. It can be folded or bent like a sheet of paper. Its durable properties make it reusable to a certain extent and infinitely repositionable when used with the proper adhesive. Once the film is removed from the surface, the repositionable artists' adhesive that holds it in place must be cleaned away from the paint with products such as RM 901 Pre-Kleeno.

- **Hand-Held Shields.** These can be used to control the airbrush spray to create stenciled shapes by spraying around their perimeter. They aid in rendering soft- and hard-edged effects.

  You can fashion your own shields or purchase any of the hundreds of commercially produced solvent-proof shields that are available in a myriad of sizes and shapes. Their multi-faceted nature makes them a time- and labor-saver. Consider them an indispensable addition to your painting toolbox.

- **Stretch Mask.** This is a very thin film that clings to metal surfaces without the use of adhesives. Once affixed to the metal, designs can be cut into it with a razor knife. A light touch is required when cutting the mask to keep from etching into the base paint. The cut-out sections are then removed to create custom stencils. Once the stretch mask is removed, no residue is evident, but the surface still should be cleaned with a cleaner-degreaser after the mask is removed.

Stretch mask is transparent and self-adhesive

- **Paint Mask.** This solvent-proof material is cut with the aid of a computer/vinyl plotter/cutter to create stencils. It has a removable backing on one side that once removed allows the computer-cut stencil to be transferred onto the painting surface with transfer tape. Each stencil is good for one use only, since the process of removing it from the surface after painting distorts it to the point of uselessness. After the paint mask is removed, its adhesive residue must be cleaned from the paint with a wax remover/degreaser, such as RM 901 Pre-Kleeno.

Paint Mask is a self-adhering computer-cut stenciling material

My Method of Stenciling.

As mentioned earlier, I consider drafting film indispensable when fashioning custom stencils. Its properties suit my painting style perfectly. Because it is rigid, it is easily handled. It can be lifted off of the surface and re-used without compromising its shape. I can pre-cut sections of the stencil before I start painting and fit them together in puzzle-like fashion. Any piece can be placed or removed multiple times to cover or uncover sections of the artwork as needed during the painting process. While it might seem complicated, this method of stenciling is very simple and offers the most control over the stencil and the image I am painting. The following is a simple exercise to demonstrate how I use drafting film to create stencils and how to use the stencils while airbrushing.

Coyote Skull Masking Exercise.

- I have drawn a coyote skull on the matte side of the drafting film with an H pencil.

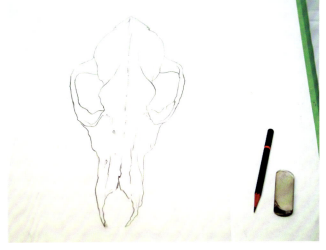

Pencil drawing on matte side of film

- The correct tool to cut the organic shape of the skull would be an electric stencil burner. I would not use an X-Acto knife, because it cuts too cleanly. I start by burning the outline of the design. This gives me two pieces.

The electric stencil burner melts instead of cuts to create a softer look

ASSORTED TIPS & WORDS OF WISDOM

Automotive airbrushing often includes painting with the aid of stencils and shields. It is recommended to spray at the lowest air pressure possible to avoid under-spray. I like the 28-35psi range.

Positive and negative stencil elements

- The eyes are next to be cut out.

The eyes are separated from the stencil with the burner

- Now there are four pieces.

Four stencil elements

- Spray a light coat of 3M spray-mount artists' adhesive on the slick side of the outline (negative) of the design and the eye cutouts.

3M artists' adhesive is sprayed onto the slick side of the drafting film

- Place the positive image on the surface to determine where the image will be painted. Note the piece of green tape on back side of the stencil to hold it in place as I arrange the other stencil pieces around it.

Place the positive stencil

- The negative is placed around the positive, glue-side down. Align the burned edges as closely as possible.

The negative stencil is placed around the positive

- The eyes are inserted glue-side down.

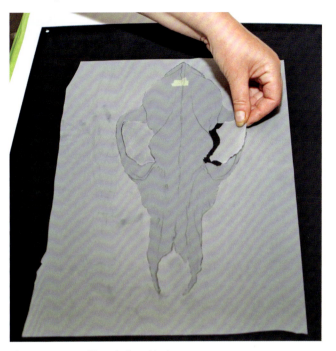

The eyes are positioned glue side down

- Remove the positive. The eyes and outline (negative) are now glued in place.

Remove the positive stencil

MASKING METHODS 55

- Mask around the area to be painted with 12" masking paper. Hold the paper in place with 3/4" 3M green masking tape.

Masking paper borders the stencil

- The Iwata Kustom CH sprays a custom-mixed light gray base color from approximately 6 inches. Use the same painting technique as described in the gradation exercise. Notice how I let the spray fill in the center and fade towards the edge. Once the stencil is lifted, the paint will have a very low edge.

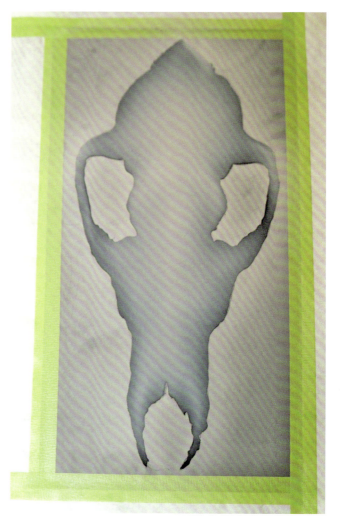

Spray a light coat of gray

- A darker middle gray is mixed.

A darker second color is mixed to spray

- The stencil burner cuts the drafting film to create shields for spraying the shadows. I follow my pencil lines.

Following pencil lines with the stencil burner

- Part of the positive is placed on the surface. Rolled green tape on its backside holds it securely onto the paint.

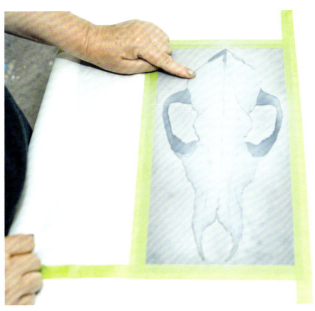
Positive stencil is positioned.

- The middle gray is sprayed in the exposed areas using the edges of the positive as a hand-held stencil to create sharp shadow.

Darker gray is airbrushed around the shield edges

- I continue to use the stencil burner to cut away sections of the positive to make shields for painting shadows and to define the shape of the skull.

The burner continues to cut the main stencil into smaller stencils

Assorted Tips & Words of Wisdom

Always use 3M tapes when masking directly on paint. The tack is perfect, it comes off of the roll easily without ripping and the fine line tapes have very crisp edges.

- After cutting, the stencil is repositioned in preparation for painting. Note that no adhesive is used on the positive.

The stencil is repositioned

- More middle gray is sprayed to define the skull using the shield.

Dark gray is sprayed to paint in the eye sockets

- The shield is eliminated, and the rest of the skull will be painted freehand, with gradations of gray and some funky dagger strokes indicate cracks and deterioration.

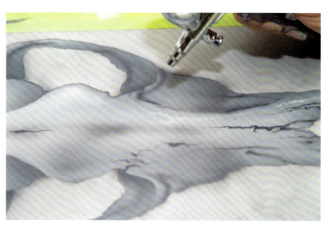

Details are airbrushed freehand

- I use the light gray to spray the highlights.

Light gray sprays the highlights

- The drafting film is removed.

The drafting film is removed

- The adhesive residue is cleaned away using RM 901 Pre-Kleeno and a paper towel.

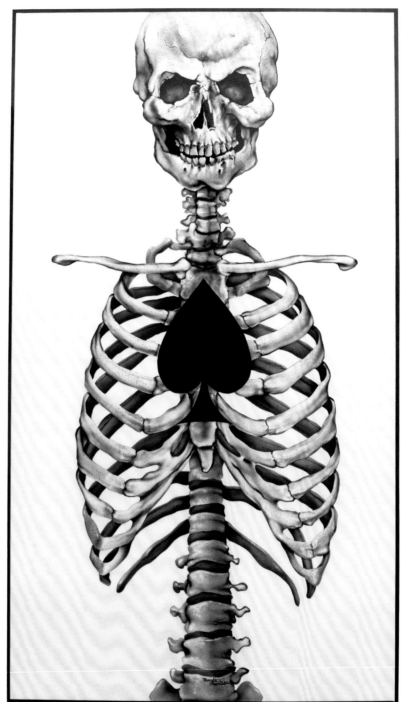

CHAPTER SEVEN

Ace of Spades Skeleton Lesson

The skeleton is an archetype that crosses all cultures. My artistic assignments often require a fresh take on the old theme. I've combined Mr. Bones with another icon (Ace of Spades) for this how-to.

This skeleton example demonstrates cutting the stencil on the surface of the paint and a vinyl plotter/cutter.

The practice of cutting on the paint saves time by eliminating some of the steps that I use when stenciling with drafting film. It does require a very light hand. If paint is etched by the cutting blade, the cut lines will be evident once the paint is clear coated and polished. The ability to cut a stencil on the paint without carving into the paint itself is one of the skills that separate great painters from good painters.

Vinyl plotter/cutters are also a great tool for saving time. Their consistent accuracy is unattainable by human means. This tool does require some computer savvy to use, but it is an indispensable asset to any custom auto painter.

The substrate is aluminum that has been painted pearl white, clear coated and wet-sanded in preparation for airbrushing. I am spraying with one color, RM Carizzma Smoke polyester dye. This is a transparent paint and should be sprayed in the same manner as a candy color.

Skeleton Example.

- I started with a sketch on 11 x 14 inch paper.

- The design has been penciled onto a 24 x 36 inch aluminum panel with the aid of a projector.

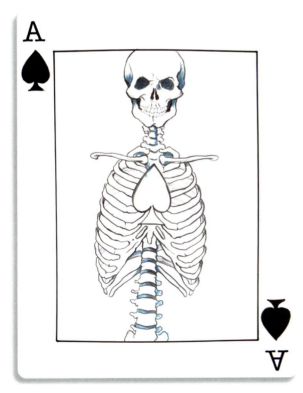

Pencil sketch

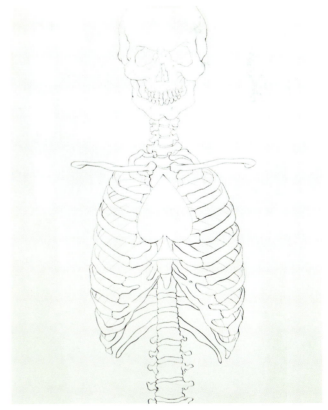

Pencil drawing on painted aluminum

- Artool Stretch Mask is employed as the stenciling agent. It is perfect for cutting on the paint, because it is very transparent and solvent-proof. Its tack is more than adequate to hold it in place and ensure against under-spray.

Stretch Mask applied

- Masking paper surrounds the borders of the panel that are not covered by the Stretch Mask. I start cutting out the areas that are to be painted first.

Perimeter is masked with paper

- Close-up of cutting the ribs on the skeleton's back with an X-Acto knife with a #11 blade.

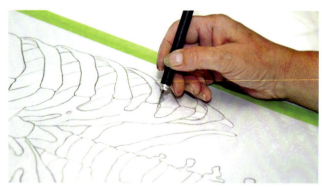

Cutting our rear rib cage

- The first round of cutting is complete and the background details are ready to be airbrushed.

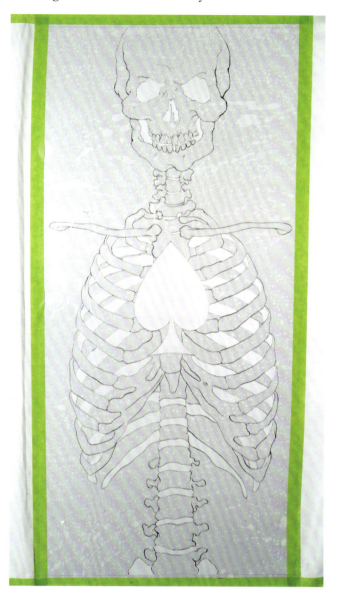

Ready to paint

- Airbrushing begins. Notice how the color gradates from the bone's edge to the middle. This will help define its round shape as I paint. This is all about lines and gradations.

Assorted Tips & Words of Wisdom

Always endeavor to deliver your best work, even if it is a small job. Your customer will appreciate the effort and you never know who might see it.

Paint is gradated from the edge to middle of bone design

- Background bones are airbrushed.

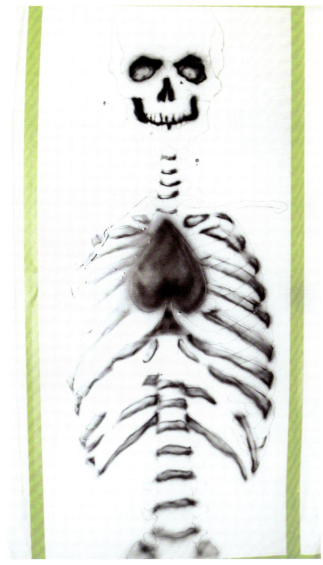

Back of rib cage painted

- Some of the neck and spine bones are unmasked.

Neck bone sections removed

- The masking is removed from the teeth.

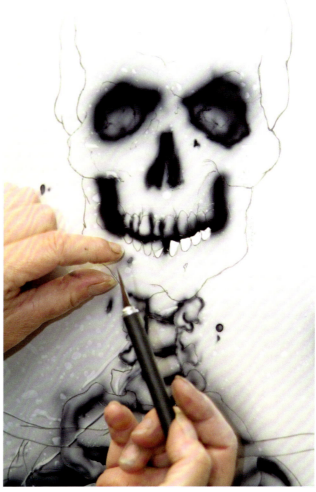

Stretch Mask is removed from the teeth

ACE OF SPADES SKELETON LESSON 63

- Teeth are painted.

Neck and teeth are detailed freehand with mini dagger strokes and gradations

- The unmasked neck and spine bones are airbrushed.

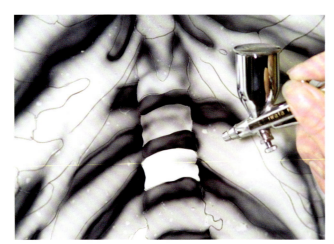

Vertebrae are airbrushed

- The masking over the jaw is cut and removed.

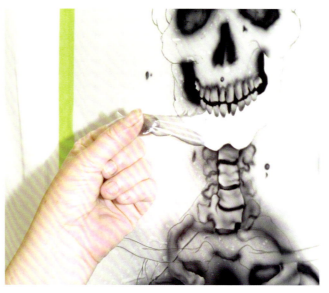

Mask is cut and removed from jaw

- Reduce air pressure with the MAC (micro air control) valve to approximately 5 psi. This creates a fine spray of dots.

Air pressure is reduced to 5 psi

- While the air pressure is reduced by the MAC valve, I paint the exposed bones with the speckle effect.

- More Stretch Mask is removed from the ribs and skull so they can be airbrushed.

Paint sprayed at a low psi renders large speckles instead of fine mist

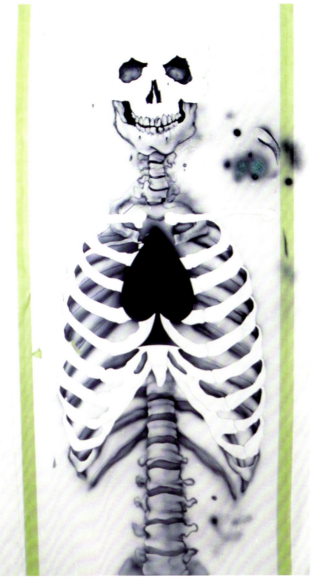

Masking is removed from the skull and foreground rib cage

Assorted Tips & Words of Wisdom

Don't be afraid to try different base colors under your transparent (candy) paints. Changing the base color will dramatically alter the color of any transparent paint that is over it. Pearls, colored metal flake and other specialty paints make great foundations for transparent colors.

- Low-pressure speckled effects are added to the skull and ribs.

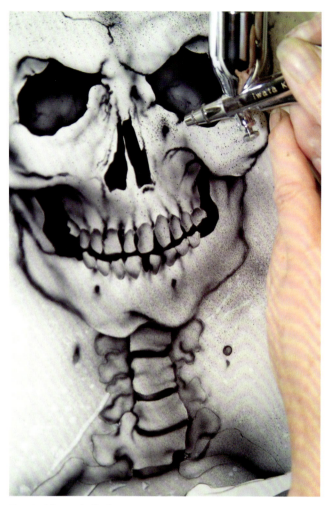

Specked low psi effect

- The airbrush is held close to the surface (1/8"), and detail is added to the bones with mini-dagger lines and color gradations. Trigger movement back and forth are minimal from this distance (trigger position 0-1-0).

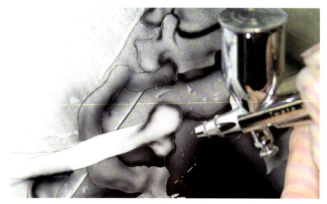

Clavicle detail

- I continue to paint down the right rib cage. The 3-D effect is becoming apparent. Notice that all detailing of the bone effects are forms of dots, lines and gradations.

Right-side rib cage

- The right-side rib cage is completely tricked-out with various controlled daggers and gradations.

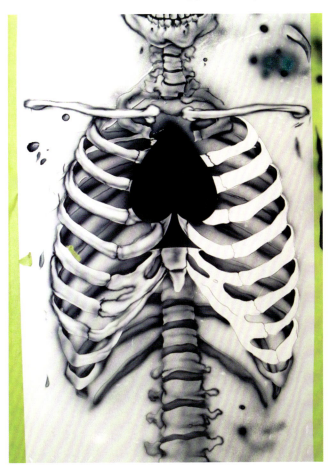

Rib cage complete

- The left rib cage is detailed in the same manner as the right side.

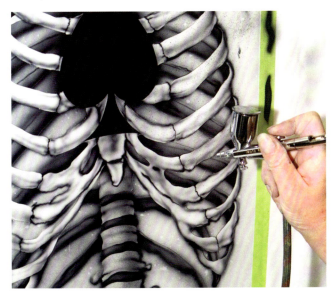

Left rib cage

- The MAC valve on the airbrush is adjusted to very low psi to produce the spatter effect.

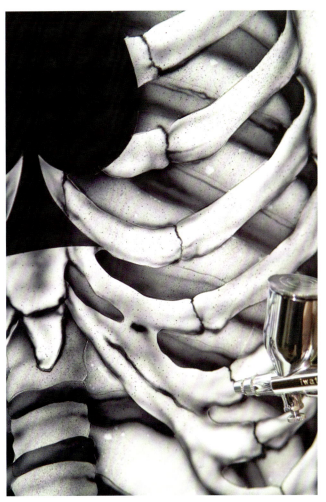

Controlled speckles

- The Stretch Mask is pulled away.

Stretch Mask is removed

- A Sakura electric eraser (one of my secret weapons) serves to pull up highlights in the art by discreetly removing paint to expose the base color.

In addition to combining dots, lines and gradations to create this image, low air pressure and erasing methods added the extra detail that was needed to jack this artwork up another notch to beyond the ordinary.

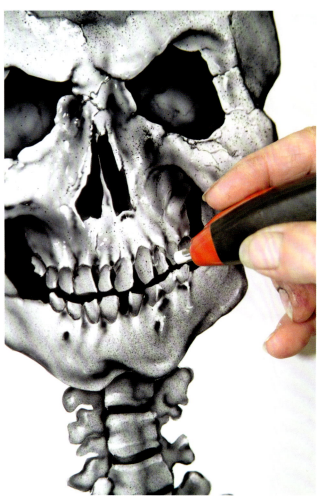

Erasure technique creates highlights

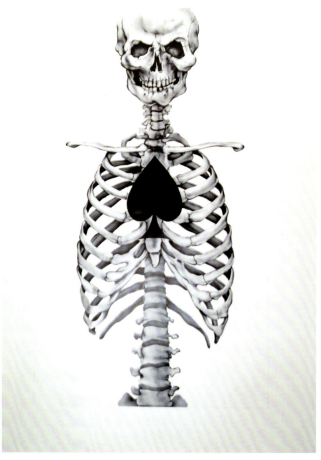

Completed skeleton

Assorted Tips & Words of Wisdom

Match the size of your airbrush or air gun to the size of the job. Don't be afraid to use a larger spray gun in the same manner as your airbrush if the job is large enough. You will save time and make more money. Just be careful not to build the paint up against the edges of any tape or masks that you employ during the course of spraying, because the larger gun will spray a larger volume of pigment when compared to the airbrush. High edges complicate the clear-coating process and can be seen in the design once the clearcoat has been sprayed.

Ace Skeleton Border Stripe "How-To."

- After looking at the finished skeleton, I realized he needed a border. Fine-line masking tape 1/8 inch wide is put down on the surface to mask a border around the skeleton. Both sides of the 1/8 inch tape are abutted with 1/4 inch fine line tape. Both sides of the 1/4 inch tape are bordered with 3/4 inch green masking tape. Masking paper protects against over-spray beyond the green masking tape and over the skeleton image. The following photos show the fine-line tape in place on the right side and the 1/8 inch tape removed from the center of the other tape for painting on the left side.

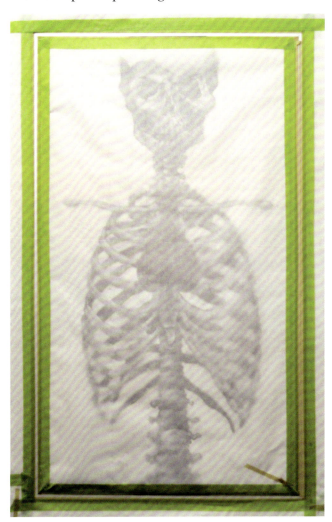

Taped out pinstripe border

- The 1/8 inch fine line tape is removed from the right side of the painting. Note the other tapes used for this exercise are visible in this close-up.

Removing the fine line tape to expose area to be painted

- The same Smoke Carizzma used to paint the skeleton is used to airbrush the border. I keep the paint profile (thickness) to a minimum by using the airbrush instead of a larger air gun.

Paint is airbrushed into tape opening

- The masking paper is removed, followed by the 3/4 inch tape.

- Completed border after cleaning the surface with RM 901 or similar cleaner/degreaser.

All masking is removed

- The 3/4 inch fine-line tape that bordered both sides of the 1/8 inch black border is pulled up.

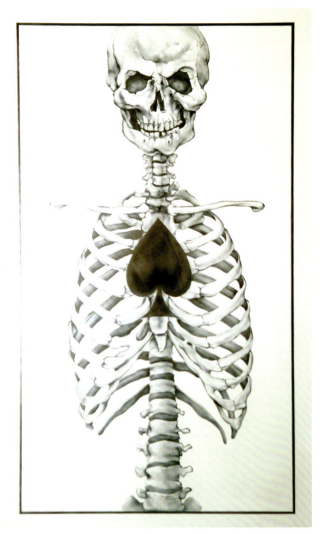

Completed project

Once the skeleton is complete, it is time to paint the letter effect and spade icon. The font style is selected, and a vinyl plotter cuts a stencil of the letter "A" out of paint mask.

Tape bordering paint is removed

Lettering Example.

- Computer-cut paint mask.

Tape is used to create a 1/2 inch spacer

- The area that is to be painted, or the "positive," is weeded from the stencil.

Positive is weeded from the design with an X-Acto knife

- Transfer tape is laid over the remaining stencil negative and squeegeed for maximum adhesion.

Transfer tape is squeegeed onto the stencil

- The excess transfer tape is trimmed off.

Excess transfer tape is trimmed from stencil

- The backing is peeled from the stencil negative to expose its adhesive backing.

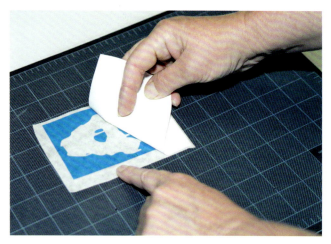
Peel backing from stencil to expose its adhesive

- At this point, the adhesive on the transfer tape and the stencil are facing the same way. The negative is positioned adhesive-side down.

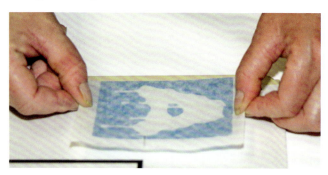
Stencil is placed on panel

- A squeegee maximizes adhesion between the paint and the stencil. Make sure to squeegee in all directions to ensure all stencil edges stick to the paint.

Squeegee aids adhesion between the stencil and the surface

- Remove the transfer tape from the stencil. Check to be sure that all inserts or other small stencil pieces are transferred to the paint and do not remain on the transfer tape.

Transfer tape is removed

- Once the area is cleaned and masked, it will be ready for painting.

Masking paper surrounds stencil

- The same transparent Smoke Carizzma color that was used for the skeleton is put in the airbrush.

- I begin spraying light passes to build the paint slowly to a dark color value. Distance to the surface is approximately 3 inches, and the trigger pull is 0-4-0 with each pass. Because the paint is transparent, I do not attempt to build the value in one or two passes, because that would require over-application of the paint, which would result in sags or drips.

Stencil painted with 6 coats of paint

Spray the first light coat of paint

- Six light coats of paint eventually build the color value I'm looking for.

- Once the masking paper is removed, the paint mask stencil can be pulled away. Go slowly, and watch the edges of the stencil as it is pulled so the painted graphics don't peel up with it.

Remove the stencil

Assorted Tips & Words of Wisdom

If your airbrush is designed to paint tiny details, the paint nozzle orifice will be very small. Small paint nozzle sizes (.18mm.-.35mm.) require less viscous paints. Over-reduce your paint until it sprays correctly. I use a 2-1 or a 3-1 ratio of reducer to paint.

- Use an X-Acto knife or other tool to pick out the inserts.

Peel up stencil inserts

- Finished letter. Make sure to clean the area with RM 901 cleaner.

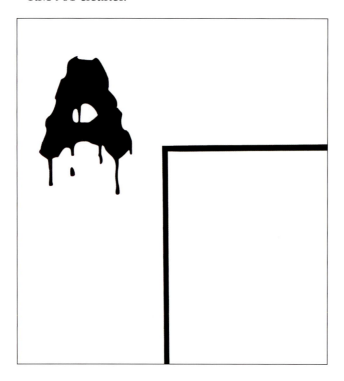

Spade Design with Plotter/Cutter

- A spade design is cut on the plotter and is painted in the same manner as the letter.

Paint-mask stencils that were cut with a vinyl plotter

- Remove the positive sections of the stencil.

The positive section is weeded from the stencil

- The stencil was applied to the panel with transfer tape and the perimeter masked out with paper.

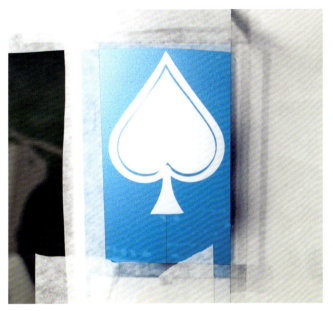

Masking paper is arranged around the area to be painted

- Airbrush the spade design. Build the color slowly over several light coats of paint. Endeavor to cover the area evenly.

Airbrush multiple light coats of paint

- Once the color value is dark enough, let the paint dry a few minutes, and remove the stencil from the surface. Immediately clean the area with RM 901.

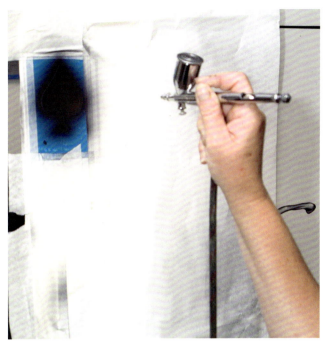

After 6 light coats of paint

- I had a bit of a problem when the stencil was pulled up. The design has a very fine line in it, and I sprayed the paint too heavy in that area. When the stencil was removed, it pulled a tiny bit of paint from the edge of the design, creating a ragged edge about 3/4 inch long.

Rough-edged area needs repairing

- The solution to fix the problem is the Artool "Big Shield." I find the contour on the shield to match the arc of the ragged edge, and repair the area.

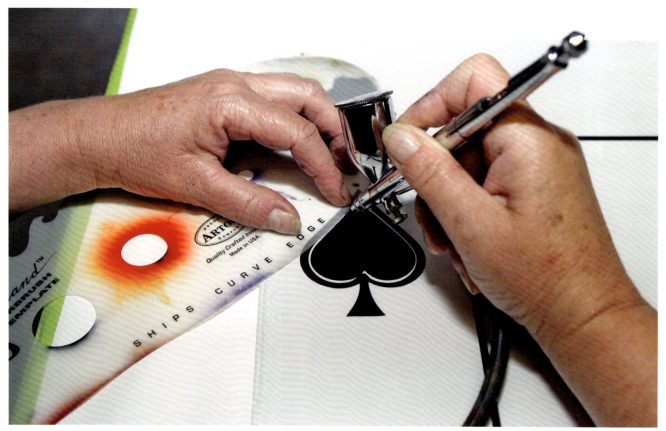

Artool "Big Shield" aids with repair

- Repaired spade.

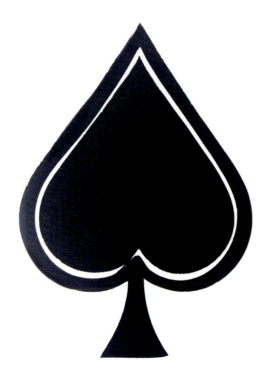

Repaired spade

ASSORTED TIPS & WORDS OF WISDOM

The further you bend over for someone, the more likely they are to "blankety-blank" you. Customers that require you to immediately drop everything to do their bidding, deliver the paint in half the time normally required, work on the cheap or all of the above, will most likely be the one who complains or creates problems when the job is delivered and it is time to pay their bill.

CHAPTER EIGHT

Tiger Bike Lesson

This mural was created for a "Born to be Wild" motorcycle promotion. It is one in a series of animal-themed cycles: a Tiger design was designated for this motorcycle. It is a perfect example of the importance of dagger strokes. The stencil openings are painted in with mini-gradations, and the details which are all forms of dots and lines, are airbrushed freehand.

I am using drafting film as a masking agent. Why? Because drafting film can be burned with the stencil burner and reused multiple times during the painting process to aid in defining the design. Why did I choose the stencil burner? An X-Acto knife could never cut with the natural organic smoothness of the burner. Any other masking method that requires cutting on the surface will not afford me this advantage.

I will be painting with RM Diamont and Carizzma paints.

- The parts are sent to me with factory paint.

- They must be re-colored black to match the frame of the motorcycle before I can begin airbrushing.

Customer parts

Parts base-coated black

Part ready to assemble on motorcycle

TIGER BIKE LESSON   79

- Once the parts return from my painter, drafting film is cut to match the size and shape of each part. I pencil the tiger-skin design onto the matte side of each piece of drafting film and match them to the appropriate cycle part.

Art is penciled onto drafting film

- I begin burning the tiger-skin design by following my pencil lines.

Stencil burner cuts by melting

- Artists' adhesive is applied lightly to the shiny side of the film. Spray the adhesive from about 12 inches away to keep from over-applying it. Leave the adhesive dry about 5 minutes to "tack up" before placing it on the metal.

Apply adhesive to shiny side of stencil

- While you are waiting for the adhesive to set, clean the part to be painted with RM 901 Pre-Kleeno.

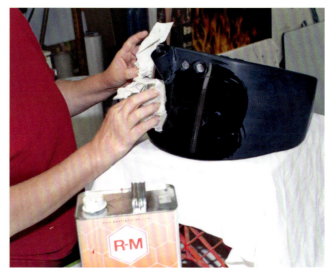

RM 901 cleans away adhesive

- Once the adhesive dries, it can be placed around the curved oil tank. Note that I cut the stencil into smaller pieces and overlap them slightly to eliminate buckling. All seams in the film are covered with 3/4 inch green masking tape.

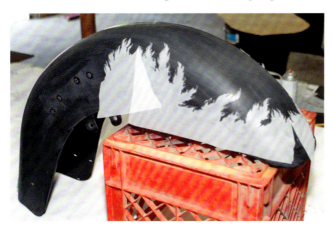

Stencil is sectioned to accommodate curvature

- Masking paper protects the rest of the part from over-spray.

Masking paper protects from over-spray

- The stencils for the remaining parts are prepared in the same manner as those just described. Lay out the art, cut or burn the design to create the stencil, apply removable adhesive, affix the stencil onto the surface to aid in airbrushing the design.

- Each stencil is matched to its appropriate part. All stencils are cut into pieces to accommodate the contours of the part. All seams in the stencil are protected with masking tape.

Stencils are positioned on their respective parts

- For the tiger face and skin on the tank, I separate the positive from the negative on the tiger face and position the positive on the tank with rolled up green tape to hold it in place. When positioning the pieces, I measure with a ruler to keep the art on both sides of the tank symmetrical.

Tiger face positioned

Assorted Tips & Words of Wisdom

Solvent based paints air dry faster, can be over-reduced and bond better to the substrate than water based paints. This property makes them my first choice when airbrushing on metal.

- The negative stencil has the adhesive sprayed onto its slick side.

Adhesive is applied to negative stencil

- Once the adhesive dries on the negative, it is cut into pieces to accommodate the curvature of the tank and adhered to the tank using the positive to determine its position. The entire design stenciled and masked.

Tiger head masked off for painting

- A Kustom TR airbrush is used to spray the white background on all of the parts. The large capacity color cup is perfect for the amount of white I need to spray.

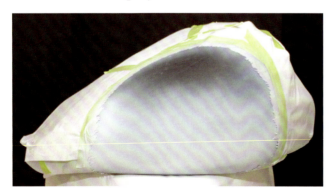

Base color sprayed with Kustom TR

- The white paint is sprayed darkest along the stencils edges and faded towards the center on the designs. I'm not too worried about even coverage, because the yellow paint that goes over it will show through differently over the various color values beneath it. The mottled effect it will create is perfect for rendering tiger fur.

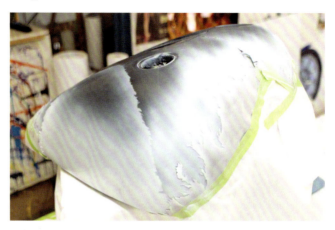

White is gradated away from the stencil's edges

- A custom-mixed yellow is added to the color cup.

Yellow is added to the color cup

Assorted Tips & Words of Wisdom

Never handle any sanded parts with bare hands, skin oils, French-fry grease or any other contaminant that can and most probably will cause problems once the clear-coat is applied.

- The yellow is airbrushed over the white and into the black base coat. Note the mottled look of the paint.

Mottled yellow

- Diamont Yellow Gold BC621 is mixed and added to the airbrush.

Custom mixed Yellow-Gold

- It is sprayed over the black and yellow to re-enforce the mottled effect. All parts are painted with the Yellow Gold.

Yellow gold airbrushed

- The eyes are burned away from the positive stencil, along with the black stripes on the tiger face.

Eyes are separated from stencil

- The positive is temporarily placed on the tank to establish the location of the eyes.

The eyes are placed

TIGER BIKE LESSON   83

- The eyes are placed to protect the eye area, and the surrounding positive is removed.

Eye stencils in place

- Adhesive is sprayed on the slick side of the positive.

Adhesive is sprayed onto the positive stencil

- Once dry, the positive is positioned on the tank.

Stencil is positioned

- Opaque Black Diamont base paint is added to the airbrush cup. Airbrush the stripes on the tiger face. Use mini dagger strokes (0-1-0) to fill in the stripe cuts.

Black tiger stripes are painted

- Remove the masking, and clean the adhesive from the tank.

Remove stencil

- A custom-mixed transparent brown (Carizzma Smoke DB24, Apple Red DB86 and Orange DB76) is sprayed to color the tiger pelt and to define the tiger's face. The trigger movement for paint application is 0-2-0 when spraying from about 8 inches from the surface. To intensify the color, I painted closer to the surface (2 inches), which required a trigger movement of 0-1-0.

Orange is gradated onto the design

- The fenders are cleaned with a tack rag and the brown is sprayed down the center of the fenders. I am staying away from masked edges.

Orange on front fender

- After tacking the parts off, Diamont base coat Deep Black is mixed and used for the black stripes on the fenders, oil tank and gas tank. They are airbrushed freehand to establish their location. I am not concerned with making them too detailed at this point, because I will come back later and tighten them up with detailed dagger strokes.

Black tiger stripes are airbrushed freehand

- Once the soft black stripes are complete, the masking is removed and adhesive cleaned away.

- Smoke Carizzma Dye, with a touch of Red Carizzma Dye to warm it up, is added to the Kustom CH. The CH is the perfect airbrush to paint the fine tiger hairs and detail the face. This part is all about the dagger strokes — thousands of them. I work on the stripes and add hairs wherever it seems natural to do so, holding the airbrush as close to the surface as possible and painting the daggers with a 0-.5-0 trigger movement.

Tiny dagger strokes detail the art

- The daggers help obscure the sharp edges so the tiger face design doesn't look cut out.

Tiger-face details

- The black dagger strokes are complete.

Black paint is complete

- RM Diamont white is airbrushed with the Kustom CH in the same manner as the black. The paint is sprayed from 1/4 inch or less from the surface and the trigger action is (0-.5-0). The goal is to soften the look of the stenciled sections with hair-like dagger strokes to "sell" the idea of tiger fur.

White highlights soften the design

- Carizzma Yellow DB65 is airbrushed lightly over select areas of white fur on the face of the cat to tone it down a bit.

- A bit of RM Carizzma Bronze powder base (PF 85) is added in with my previously custom mixed Carizzma Orange and sprayed over the center of each piece to give the colors an iridescent quality.

Bronze Carizzma powder base (PF-85) is lightly dusted onto the parts

Assorted Tips & Words of Wisdom

When applied properly, airbrushing should not be able to be felt once it has been clear-coated.

86 CHAPTER EIGHT

- Completed parts, ready for clear coating.

Parts ready for clear coat

- The parts are cleaned with a tack rag and RM 901 Pre-Kleeno in preparation for clear coating.

- Motorcycle parts require the paint and clear coat to be sprayed from all angles to build adequate coverage over their entire surface. Remember to maintain a constant distance from the surface when spraying.

3 coats of clear coat are applied

- 3 coats of clear coat provide plenty of protection and will buff to a high gloss finish. About 10 minutes of dry time between coats of clear were required.

- Once the clear-coated parts are dry, they are wet-sanded with 1500-grit paper to remove any blemishes. A second round of wet-sanding with 2500-grit paper removes the scratch marks created by sanding with the 1500 grit.

Sanding with 1500 and 2500 grit sandpaper smooths the clear coat for polishing

- Polishing compound is squirted onto the clear coat and buffed out with the electric buffer equipped with a wool polishing pad.

Polishing compound applied with a wool buffing pad

- A super-fine polishing glaze is applied with the electric buffer equipped with a foam polishing pad to complete the finishing process.

Glazing compound works best with a foam buffing pad

Born to be Wild — *The Tiger Bike*

CHAPTER NINE

Ghost King Lesson

When I began contemplating a King of Diamonds for my playing card deck, I kept thinking of the Ghost King character from the "Lord of the Rings" movie *Return of the King*. With those images as inspiration, I've devised a lesson using my own version of the Ghost King.

In this demonstration I want to show you ghosting. Ghosting buries the art under multiple layers of transparent paint. While this project includes a number of airbrush techniques, it is built on the three airbrushing basics: the dot, the line and gradation. Drafting film will be used as masking and fashioned into custom stencils to aid the painting process.

- A pencil sketch of the Ghost King of Diamonds forms the basis of the mural. I like to do a color sketch before painting to decide on my color choices before I trace the design on drafting film. An oozing letter "K" and diamond icon will be added after the main character is airbrushed.

Drawings help plan out colors and layout

- The design is drawn onto the matte-finished side of the drafting film with an H pencil.

Transferring design to matte side of the drafting film

- The foreground (positive) is separated from the background (negative).

Separate positive stencil from the negative

GHOST KING LESSON 91

- Adhesive is lightly sprayed onto the slick side of the positive stencil. I waited about 5 minutes for it to tack up enough to place it on the base paint.

Adhesive is sprayed lightly onto shiny side of drafting film

- The positive stencil (face and helmet) is placed.

Positive stencil is positioned

- The background stencil is cut into three pieces for ease of handling.

Negative is cut into 3 pieces for handling purposes

- The stencil burner separates some of the key background elements that are to be ghosted from the negative stencils. The burner renders a perfect "imperfect" edge for the cut outs, which softens the painted edge.

Stencil burner cuts away details to be painted from background (negative) stencil

- Once I am ready to place the negative stencil, it is held in position with masking tape only. Because no glue is used, the resulting underspray will soften the edges of the cut-outs.

92   CHAPTER NINE

Background stencil is placed on panel

- Smoke Carizzma straight from the can is lightly airbrushed into the background cut-outs Trigger control is 0-3-0 from about 8" from the surface.

Background skulls are airbrushed

- All three stencil negatives have the eyes, noses and other key features burned away from the stencil so they can be positioned and painted once the stencil is taped or held in place on the paint. Essentially, I am making my own custom hand-held shields as I paint along.

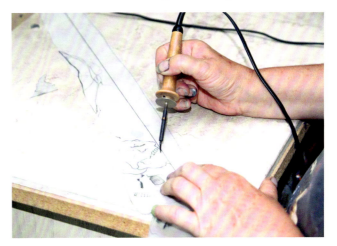

All details on negative stencil are burned out

- Japanese art paper is great to spray through to get special effects. A piece of Ogura Lace paper is hung with masking tape over the entire painting. The same Smoke Carizzma is airbrushed through the paper to augment the skulls and the entire background area. I hold the airbrush 1/4 to 1/2 inch from the surface and spray with a 0-2-0 trigger movement.

Swiss cheese-patterned paper is used as a stencil

GHOST KING LESSON 93

- Background with the Swiss cheese paper removed.

Ogura Lace Japanese Paper with Swiss cheese holes is lifted

- Transparent Teal Carizzma dye (DB 45) is gradated over the background to begin the ghosting process. I am using Iwata Kustom CH to spray the dye, because I want to selectively darken areas. In this ghosting situation, I do not want an even coverage of the gradation, since I want the background skulls to be ghosted to different degrees. I went over the background twice with the teal to make it dark enough to suit my taste. I left the upper area of the background teal-free.

Teal background color is airbrushed

- DB 48 Blue Carizzma dye is gradated on the background from the top down. The color extends from the teal-free area into the teal below.

- DB 38 Fuchsia is airbrushed over the blue onto the top corners of the background. I paint downward to the lowest border the king's crown.

Blue is gradated from top to middle of the background

- Once the blue has dried, I cut the crown from the face stencil with the X-Acto knife and remove the crown to expose the white pearl base color. Pre-Kleeno is used to clean adhesive residue from the crown area.

The crown section is separated from the positive stencil

- Spray adhesive is applied to the remaining background stencil. After waiting a few minutes for the adhesive to set up, the stencil is aligned on the panel to mask the edges of the crown. The remainder of the panel is masked off with paper.

Surrounding area is masked out to protect from over-spray

- RM Diamont Gold Aluminum (CB 66V) is used to paint the base color for the crown. Because I am painting a base and not airbrushing details, I am reducing the paint 1-1 with Glasurit normal reducer 352-91.

- The Kustom CM gradates the paint onto the pearl base. I am not attempting to cover the area evenly from edge to edge. The crown has to appear curved, so I paint the colors more intense in some areas.

Gold Aluminum is added

- The stencil burner cuts out the details of the crown stencil.

Crown details are burned out with stencil burner

GHOST KING LESSON

- The crown stencil is affixed to the surface.

Crown stencil is placed

- A copper-tinted gold is mixed by adding Orange Carizzma DB 76 to the Gold Aluminum. The color is airbrushed through the stencil cuts to render the crown details.

Gold is airbrushed through stencil

- The stencil is removed and the area is cleaned with 901.

Remove the stencil

- A section of the crown stencil is cut away to aid in the creation of a beveled edge.

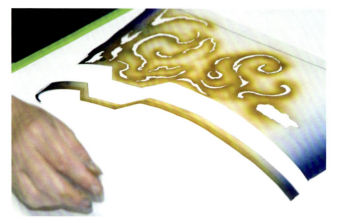

Crown stencil is divided into 2 stencils

- The stencil is replaced on the surface and the bottom edge of the crown is airbrushed with the aid of the stencil's edge.

Crown's edge is defined utilizing stencil

- The stencil is removed and surface cleaned.

Stencil is pulled away

- The copper gold is gradated onto the rear of the crown to give it some curvature. Trigger control is 0–6–0 at 6 inches away from the surface.

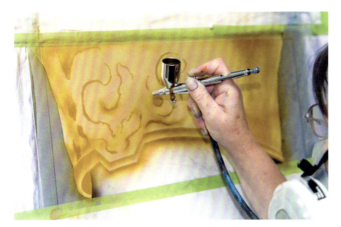
Gold is airbrushed onto select areas to define the shape

- Two coats of the DB 65 are sprayed evenly over the crown area. The details are starting to become obscured by the paint that is ghosting them.

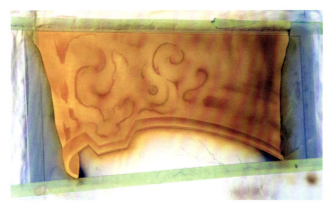
Details are ghosted under 2 coats of gold

- The crown details are further softened with freehand airbrushing so they don't look stenciled.

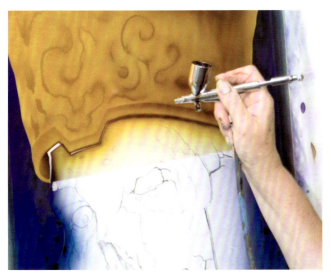
Details are enhanced with freehand airbrushing

- I add a small amount of Dark Gold that I had to the copper gold and continue to paint freehand until I get the color values right on the crown, so they look good when they are ghosted in the next step with Carizzma Yellow dye base DB 65.

- The background stencil has been removed, and a dark brown Carizzma mix is airbrushed onto the crown to further establish its shape.

More freehand detailing

- The stencil covering the face area is pulled up to expose the white pearl base color.

- The face stencil is repositioned onto the base color. Now the side sections are ready to paint.

Remove stencil

- The two sections that border the face are separated from the stencil.

Remaining positive stencil is placed

Positive stencil is cut into pieces

Assorted Tips & Words of Wisdom

Never let anyone else determine how much your work is worth or how much they will pay you for a job. Set your own prices based on the assignment and make no excuses.

- RM Yellow BC 605 base coat is airbrushed into the two sections. I paint some areas darker than others by building up more paint. The result will help define the shape and texture of the garment.

Yellow is painted into the exposed areas

- A custom mixed dark brown is airbrushed through a fabric softener sheet to render a decrepit textured effect.

Fabric softener sheet is used as a stencil to add texture

- Freehand airbrushing adds the shadow effects. The shadows are a combination of dagger strokes and mini-gradations.

Area is further detailed with freehand airbrushing

- The features of the face stencil are burned out with the stencil burner.

Facial features cut out with stencil burner

- The stencil is positioned on the face with the mouth, nose and eye sockets exposed for painting.

Stencil is positioned on panel

- Diamont BC 850 is airbrushed into the stencil openings. Notice that this is all lines and mini-gradations.

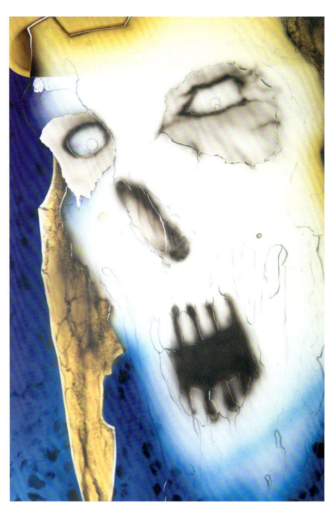

Features are painted with the aid of stencil

- More stencil material is burned away from the face stencil to make edges that will be used to paint the facial shape and decrepit details. Some of the teeth are removed from the stencil so they can be painted, as well.

More details are cut away from the positive stencil

- The stencil is positioned on the panel. The white areas have been cleaned and are ready to paint.

Stencil is placed and ready to paint through

- More BC 850 is airbrushed to detail the face.

The teeth and other details are painted using stencil

- The stencil is removed.

Stencil is removed

Assorted Tips & Words of Wisdom

It is always better to cover-up than to clean-up. Take the time to protect adjacent areas from paint over-spray. You will not regret it.

Ghost King Lesson 101

- Shadows and contours are airbrushed freehand with a combination of lines and gradations.

- More freehand airbrushing details the teeth, cheeks and the area around the eyes.

More facial details are added freehand

More detailing

- The air pressure is reduced with the MAC valve (Micro Air Control — available on select Iwata airbrushes) to approximately 5 psi. This causes the airbrush to spray grainy dots instead of a mist.

- I mixed up some yellow base paint with white and a drop of purple and tan to create a putrescent skin tone. The color is gradated over the facial features to re-enforce and enhance their look.

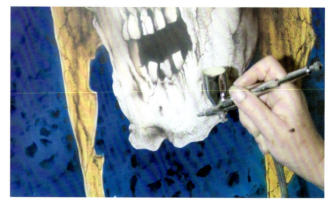

Air pressure reduced with the MAC valve

Skin tone is enhanced with custom color

- The stencils are removed from the eyes. The dark brown details the eyes and adds the eyeballs and pupils. I paint over some of the dark areas to make them darker.

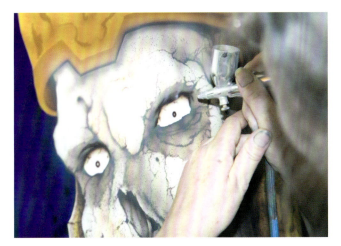

Eyes and other details are painted

- Fuchsia Carizzma is gradated over the helmet, eyes and skin to warm up the entire design.

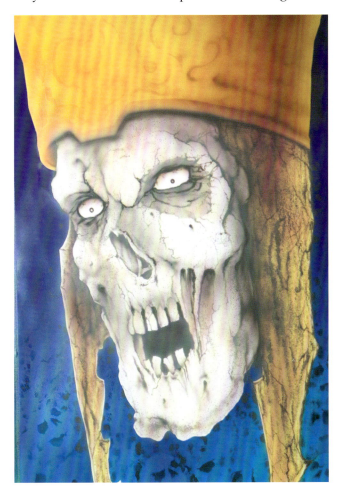

Fuchsia is gradated over facial features

- Teal is airbrushed into the whites of the eyes.

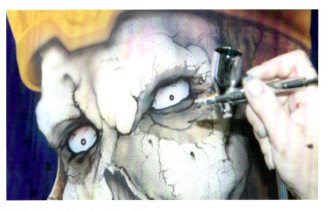

Teal is airbrushed into the whites of the eyes

- The border masking tapes and paper are removed.

- Now is the time for one of my super-secret techniques. A fiberglass eraser deftly removes paint to expose the white base paint and create the highlights. This makes more detail with less paint. The fiberglass eraser is from Ampersand Art Products. It is part of their Claybord tool kit.

Fiberglass eraser kicks up the detail

- This panel will be completed by adding a "K" and a diamond icon in two of the corners. The painting sequence is the same as the "A" and spade icon in the Spade Skeleton lesson.

Once the clear coat is sprayed over the panel and dried, it can be buffed to a high gloss.

CHAPTER TEN

Draco Exercise

In keeping with the Icons of Automotive airbrushing theme, I will render "Draco," which means Dragon. These mythological beasts have long been associated with power, wisdom, creation and destruction. I hold a special connection with the spirit of the Dragon since creation and destruction also fall within the purview of the artist. In this image Draco is creating a universe where he will rule by employing both power and subtle beauty.

This panel is intended to be an integral part of BASF's display at the SEMA automotive show in Las Vegas, Nevada. It will not only showcase my airbrushing skills, but also the awesome paint effects made possible with RM and Carizzma paints. Because of the scope and scale of the project, this is quite possibly the longest how-to lesson for custom automotive airbrushing in print. Enjoy!

---

1. I started with a pencil sketch to work out the design scheme.

2. After I'm happy with the rough, I do a color rendition with colored pencils to determine which colors of paint need to be mixed up before I start painting the mural.

3. After the color version is complete, the black-and-white version is projected to scale onto the matte side of a 3 x 5 foot piece of drafting film. A 2B drawing pencil is perfect for tracing the outlines of the dragon with the aid of the projector.

4. A stencil burner separates the drago (positive) stencil from the background (negative) stencil by burning an organic looking edge on the stencils.

5. The 3 x 5 foot steel panel was base-coated with a deep black base color.

6. As always, the panel is cleaned with RM 901 cleaner before any taping, masking or painting.

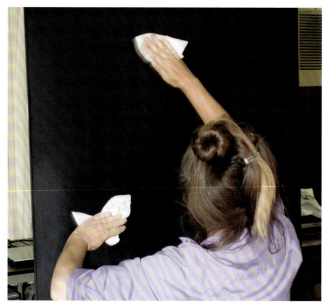

7.   I use pieces of green 3/4 inch masking tape that are rolled into small "sticky side-out loops" to hold the positive stencil into place on the metal. This will help me eyeball the perfect location to place the dragon by allowing me to reposition the stencil numerous times until I get it just where I want it.

8.   I flip the negative so its shiny side is facing up on a clean surface. 3M repositionable adhesive is lightly sprayed over the cut edges of the negative stencil. I save glue and clean-up hassles by focusing the adhesive spray only on the edges where the paint will abut the stencil. Less glue sprayed means less glue to clean up later.

9.   After spraying the adhesive, invert the can and evacuate all of the glue from the nozzle. This will ensure that the tip will not clog. Let the adhesive tack-up for about five minutes before handling.

10.   I then cut the negative into smaller pieces with an X-Acto knife so the pieces are easier to handle. The pieces of the negative stencil are placed around the positive. Every piece is matched to its counterpart on the positive stencil. Each seam in the negative is covered with 3/4 inch green masking tape.

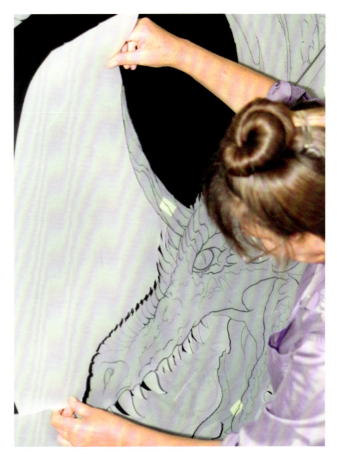

11. Masking tapes in widths of 3/4 and 2 inch in addition to 12 inch masking paper are used to mask off the background areas that are not to be painted yet. A Dragon is ready to be born.

12. The positive stencil is laid down with the shiny side up. It is cut into 3 sections, the neck, the head and a gill plate.

13. The sections are arranged shiny side up in preparation for the adhesive spray application.

14. 3M repositionable adhesive is sprayed very lightly from 8 to 10 inches over the entire stencil. This is different from step 8 where only the edges are sprayed. The reason is that the entire positive stencils will be reused multiple times during the painting process to continually cover and uncover specific areas that are being airbrushed. The adhesive will lose a bit of tack each time it is applied to the surface and lifted off. With a little practice you will learn exactly how much adhesive to spray and how long it will work for you without reapplying the glue.

Assorted Tips & Words of Wisdom

If you airbrush on large areas, you need to regularly stand back and take a "long look" at the color and composition of it as you paint. It is the only way to truly view the image as most viewers will see it.

15. The glue is dry. I want to protect the neck from overspray when I paint the face, so I position the neck stencil to mask it off. A piece of masking paper covers the area of the background that the stencil does not in order to protect it from over-spray.

16. I have to cover the inside of the mouth to protect it from the green over-spray also. That means I have to separate the teeth, tongue and cheek from the main stencil.

17. The newly separated pieces are positioned to mask their specific areas. I use green masking tape to cover any slightly mismatched edges where the stencils butt together.

18. The entire mouth area is masked off.

19. I take time to clean the face area one more time with the 901.

20. A custom mixed Diamont Yellow-Green is sprayed through an Iwata Kustom HI-Line TH airbrush. The TH airbrush comes with two spray heads. One sprays an oval pattern and the other sprays a round pattern. For rendering murals, I prefer the round spray pattern so I am using the round spray head.

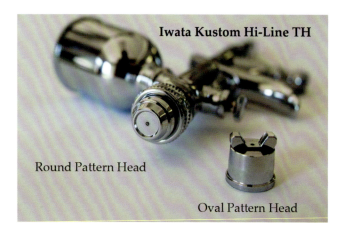

21. The color is airbrushed more intensely on the stencil edges to give them some punch.

22. The airbrush is held anywhere from 1/2 to 3 inches from the surface depending on how tight I want to paint in the details.

23. I paint away from the edges with various gradations to build the base color of the lizard-skin color.

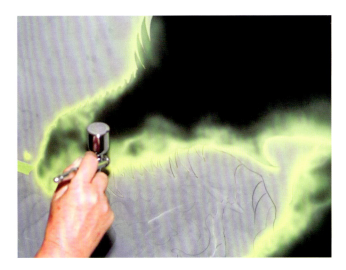

24. I'm going to define the eye now, so I need to determine its position. I cut the eye away from the face stencil.

25. The face stencil is positioned using the stencils around it as a guide. With the face stencil in place, the eye can be base-painted through the eyehole.

26. The face stencil is removed. The eye base color is apparent.

27. The entire face area is cleaned of adhesive residue with 901.

28. With the eye in place, more green is sprayed into the face to begin to define the brow and shape of the finned head.

DRACO EXERCISE   111

29. The spiny appendages are cut away from the main stencil with the X-Acto knife to render a crisp cut as opposed to a softer organic cut from a stencil burner.

30. The main positive stencil is repositioned so the newly cut spiny stencils can be registered accurately on the surface.

31. Positioning the spines.

32. The main stencil is pulled away, leaving the spine stencils properly positioned to protect their area from over-spray.

33. The section of the eye that was cut away is placed on the surface to mask it off.

34. I mixed up a slightly darker green color and add it to the airbrush color cup.

35. Before painting, I use the tack rag to remove any dust.

36. The Iwata Kustom HI-Line TH airbrush sprays the paint over the large area efficiently. I use the color the same way as the first green. I am not creating details, just building various color values over the face area. It is a mottled base color that will act as under-painting for the airbrushed details.

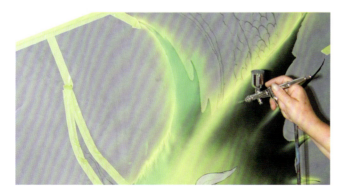

37. I put Carizzma DB-45 Teal color into my Kustom CH airbrush. A touch of Carizzma powder base PF54 is also added to the paint to add a hint of opal marine into the color. I am changing to the Kustom-CH airbrush to paint the level of detail required for this image. I am personally more comfortable with the standard airbrush trigger position being on the top of the airbrush as opposed to the pistol-grip version when painting smaller details.

38. The stencil burner separates the eye socket area from the main stencil along with the nostril and the scale ridges of the brow.

39. The remaining positive face stencil is positioned along with the gill plate portion of the stencil.

40. The teal is airbrushed along the freshly cut and placed edges of the stencils. These include the lower jaw, gill plate, eye socket and brow ridge.

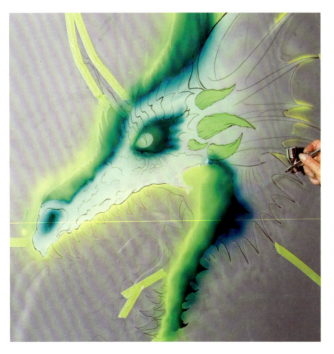

41. I have an option at this point — I can cut the drafting film that depicts the scaly ridges from the brow to the muzzle area into pieces and spray each scale individually. This would be time consuming, so instead I am opting to freehand paint the scales instead of stenciling them. The same teal color is used to paint the ridges and scales.

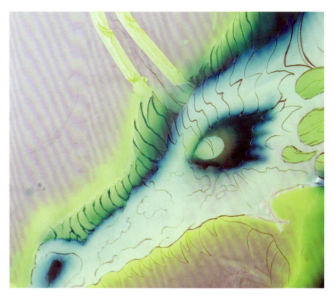

42. The lower jaw will be painted differently, I am going to cut its stencil into pieces to give that part of the painting a little more punch. Since I never want my airbrushing to appear cut out, I will still freehand over the stenciled edges to disguise the cut edge. Here I am cutting up the lower jaw stencil with the stencil burner.

Assorted Tips & Words of Wisdom

When painting on a ladder, your hourly rate or job estimate should be 50% more than your normal fee would be. Painting on the ceiling requires that you double what you would normally charge. The time and effort to paint in these situations will slow you down and take their toll on your body. If the customer questions the charges, let them try to hold an airbrush steady while painting over their head for 5 minutes — no more explanations will be required.

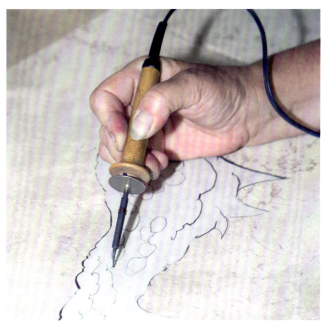

43. The stencil for the edge of the dragon's mouth is placed.

44. The same teal is airbrushed along the edge of the stencil from 1/2 inch away with 0-1-0 dagger strokes. This is not a precise operation. The idea is to create a mottled effect that will resemble dragon scales.

45. The stencil is removed from the surface and

I am pointing to the painted edge. I will alter its appearance with freehand detailing at a later point.

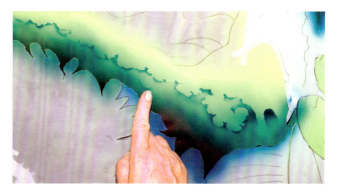

46. The other pieces of the jaw stencil are positioned and their edges are painted with the same dagger strokes as the previous step.

47. The jaw stencil is removed. All of the remaining detail on the jaw will be done freehand. The airbrush will be held 1/4 inch or closer to the surface for the freehand painting and the trigger motion will be minute. (0 -.25-0). Freehand details consist on tiny teal colored lines and gradations that accentuate the stenciling and mottled base color. I like to extend some of the stenciled landmarks to satisfy my whimsy and add a bit of flair where I feel it needs it.

48. The same type of detailing that I did on the lower jaw needs to be done on this spiny gill appendage. While the jaw details are sort of jumbled, these details will be more linear. The freehand appointments on the gill and jaw fade out into the darker shadowed areas below them.

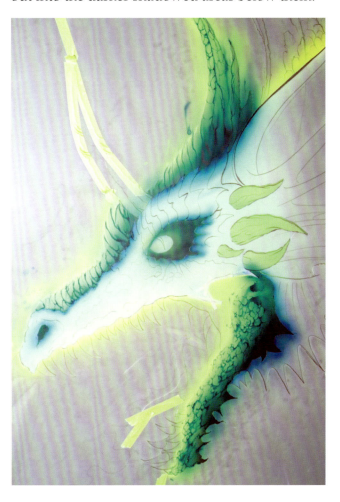

49. More mini dagger lines will be added to the ridge of the snout so it will emulate the details of the other areas. The shadows are reinforced and the details are blended out into the shadows.

Assorted Tips & Words of Wisdom

Changing colors on the vehicle with transparent and special-effect paints is a great way to save time and create unique effects.

50. Moving my attention to the eye, I cut the eye stencil into two parts.

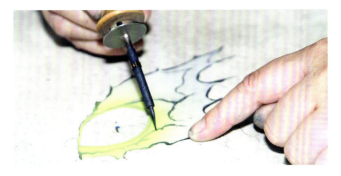

51. The eye stencils are placed on the surface.

52. RM Diamont BC 838 Magenta is put into the airbrush.

53. I paint the magenta along the edges of the eye stencil.

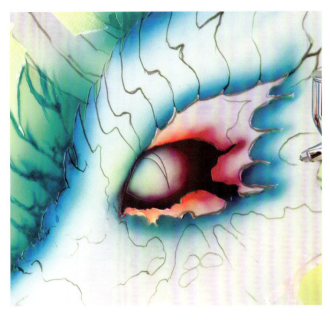

54. The eye stencils are pulled up.

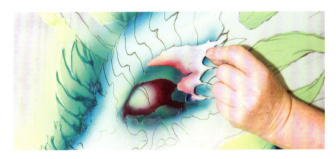

55. The face stencil is removed. Clean the surface as necessary with a tack rag or 901 if the stencils leave any adhesive residue once they are pulled up.

56. The remaining face stencil will now be cut apart with the stencil burner and X-Acto knife to help in rendering the dragon's face. I will start cutting the eyebrow apart with the stencil burner.

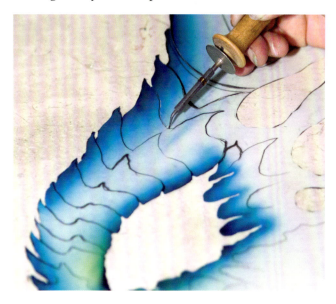

57. I have separated each section of the eyebrow and arranged them in order on a piece of cardboard.

58. Each section or scale is positioned on the panel in order. Now, with the stencil pieces in place, all that I need to do is paint and peel my way down the eyebrow.

59. The magenta is cleaned from the airbrush and teal is put into the color cup. A series of tiny dagger strokes follows the cut edge of the stencil. I use a tiny gradation to fade the color away from the stencil edge. Because the stencil has been reused so many times, the tack of the adhesive that I sprayed on it is almost gone. In some cases, I must use my left index finger to hold the stencil in place while I am spraying due to the low tack factor on the stencil. I like the low tack because it leaves no residue on the surface once it is lifted.

60. Completed eyebrow.

61. The upper maw of the face stencil will now be burned apart into many smaller stencils that I will piece together and use to airbrush the landmark details of the face. The landmark details will be accentuated with freehand airbrushing to complete the effect.

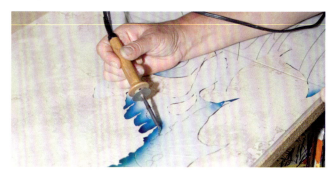

62. The Stencil of the maw is properly positioned on the surface.

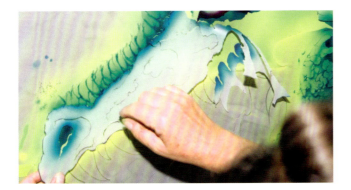

63. I start off by airbrushing along its edge. I keep tight to the surface to intensify the color (approximately 1/4 inch).

64. As I progress downward, I will gradually spray from a further distance from the surface to create a softer looking edge (approximately 6 inches).

65. Now is a good time to add the shadows of the dragon's horns with this color. These have been masked out earlier.

66. I've cut some hinged windows in the maw stencil so I can pull the window open to expose the area for painting and close the window to recover the area when I paint adjacent to it. I aim the teal paint directly onto the stencil edge and gradate it away to nothing as I progress towards the center of the opening.

67. My left hand holds part of the nostril stencil away so I can airbrush the nostril's edge to indicate its location.

68. All of the maw and nostril stencil material is removed. Because the stencil has been lifted and reused so many times, there was glue residue to clean away before I start freehand airbrushing in the details.

69. A combination of tiny dots, lines and gradations serve to enhance the shadows, increase the texture and further define the shape of the beast's maw. Since the teal Carizzma paint I am using is transparent, it is a simple matter to build the color to any value that I wish it to be. This enables me to render many variations in the look and effect of the paint while only painting with one color.

70. Freehand detail complete.

71. The stencil burner separates the spines from the webbing on the stencil that comprises the fan-like appendage on the side of the dragon's face.

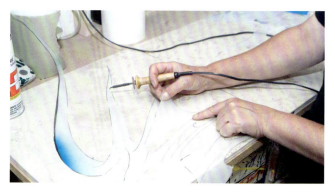

72. I notice that I need more chartreuse color in the underpainting for the area that I am preparing to airbrush. I put some of the color into the airbrush and paint it into the area.

73. Once the paint has dried, I use a tack rag to pick up any loose paint particles. The stencils that represent the spines are positioned by fitting them against the adjacent stencil's edge.

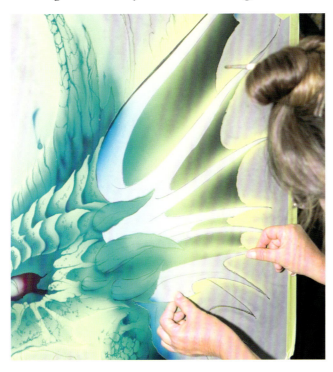

74. To begin painting, I mix up an opaque warm orange color and start painting the webbing that is between the spines. Starting on the outside edges, I airbrush the orange very dark on the edges and mottle it as I gradate away from the edge. I use the term *mottle* to indicate that this is not a smooth, even gradation. The uneven mottled look will help sell the idea of bumpy uneven skin. What is nice about these custom colors is that since the paint does not require a catalyst, I can save them indefinitely for use on another job.

75. The orange paint is blasted on with a 0-10-0 trigger travel with the airbrush being held at 12 inches from the surface. The orange fades out into the green of the webbing. Using the same color, I move in very close to the surface and use tiny trigger movements (0-1-0) to create pale vein-like lines.

76. I cleaned the airbrush and added an opaque bright yellow Diamont base color BC 655 to the airbrush's color cup.

77. The veins are extended into the orange and green areas of the webbing. These veins are simply lines of various widths. This step really begins to add some texture to the artwork.

78. 1.5 ounces of transparent Carizzma Yellow has about 1/4 teaspoon of Sunfire Gold powder base (PF68) added to it.

79. The mixture is painted over the entire area of the webbing. Paint by making overlapping passes to ensure adequate coverage.

80. Orange Carizzma (DB76) is airbrushed over the outer edges of the webbing to reinforce the orange in the area.

81. The stencils covering the spines are removed.

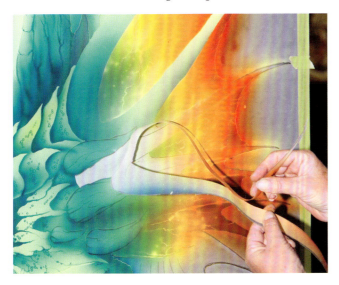

82. A dark opaque yellow is put into the airbrush and painted into the spines.

83. The airbrush is cleaned out and a light opaque yellow is added. The color will blend from the dark yellow into the green. I build some reflected light onto the spines with more tiny daggers and gradations.

84. The same light yellow highlights the scales on the muzzle of the beast. Note that these highlights are just dagger strokes, nothing more.

85. I continue to detail the face with a series of dots and daggers to add 3-D effects.

86. The stencil that is covering the throat area is pulled up.

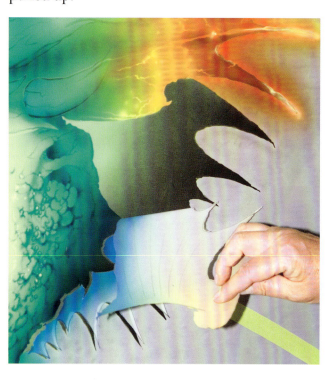

87. Since the stencil that was covering the throat area left some adhesive residue, I clean the glue away with 901. Use your fingers to feel for sticky spots after you have cleaned to make sure you have removed all of the glue.

88. Now is also a good time to pull up the neck stencil. The area the stencil was covering is cleaned with 901.

89. The gill/spine stencil is replaced to mask off the edge between the orange and yellow areas and the blue color that is going to be sprayed next. I also use masking paper to extend the over-spray protection. Then I reposition a portion of the lower jaw stencil because I will be spraying blue into that area, and I need its edge to indicate where the jaw ends and the gill begins.

90. A custom opaque turquoise color is mixed to spray onto the neck and throat area.

91. Painting begins in the throat area.

92. The jaw stencil is pulled away once the throat has been colored to expose the parts of the jaw that require blue paint.

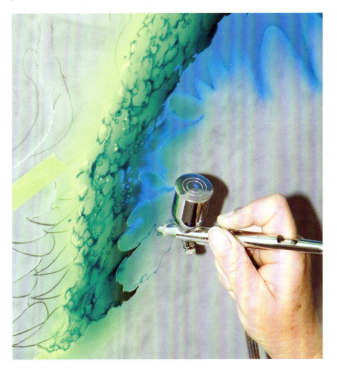

93. Blue daggers and lines add the detail to the jaw.

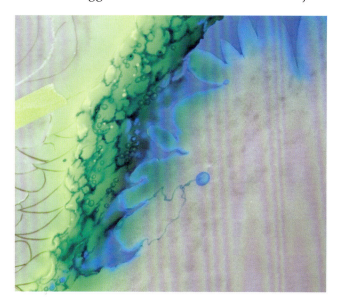

94. The spines on the neck are airbrushed turquoise and the color is gradated to fade out in the black background color of the neck.

95. The airbrush is cleaned of the turquoise color and opaque ultramarine blue is added to the color cup.

96. The color is gradated into the throat area. I will hold the airbrush closer to add details at several points in the spraying process to indicate folds and shadows.

97. The same process is done on the neck area. For this large area I am pulling the trigger in a 0-10-0 action to deliver the most paint. The blue fades out into the black.

Assorted Tips & Words of Wisdom

If you have the space, trick-out your paint shop with a good stereo system, a DVD player and possibly cable television. Those long hours painting can be more relaxing with your favorite tunes or movies to get you in the creative mode.

98. The airbrush is held closer to the surface to paint in smaller details on the back spines and to render a scaly look to the skin.

99. While the blue is in the airbrush, I freehand details around the eye and nose areas. The shadows at the base of the back spines are also freehand painted.

100. The blue is removed from the airbrush and an opaque yellow is added to the color cup. The stencil burner cuts the belly section away from the neck stencil.

101. The neck stencil is repositioned in order to expose the belly region for painting. I use masking paper to protect the adjacent areas.

102. The belly is airbrushed opaque yellow with lines, dots and little gradations. After spraying, the paint is evacuated from the airbrush.

103. Transparent Yellow Carizzma DB65 with the PF68 powder base mixed in is airbrushed over the opaque yellow in the belly area. Trigger motion is 0-10-0 from a distance of 12 inches.

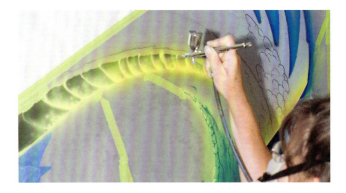

104. After spraying, the airbrush color cup is cleaned out and the Diamont Magenta is added to the color cup. Because this color has been around the shop awhile, I strain the paint to eliminate any dried paint flecks or other foreign materials. I also over-thinned the paint to 4 parts reducer to 1 part paint so it would blend transparently into the other colors.

105. The masking stencils and paper are removed from the throat, neck and gill areas. I can feel some adhesive on the surface, so I clean the entire area with 901. I rub lightly because the 901 will remove paint if you rub too hard when the cleaner is still wet on the surface.

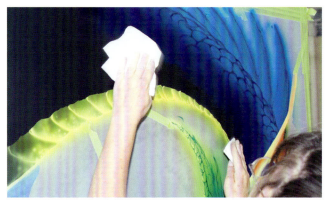

106. After the Yellow Carizzma on the belly is dry, I reposition the stencil that matches it in order to mask off the yellow belly from the magenta that will be sprayed adjacent to it.

107. The magenta is gradated from the belly up into the blue color on the back. It is difficult to see the magenta against the black background until it is clear coated. The color can be readily seen on the masking stencil that covers the belly. The over-thinned paint must be sprayed slowly to build the color value. The trigger action is 0-10-0 from a 12 inch distance.

108. While the magenta is in the airbrush, I use it to detail the webbing on the face with tiny lines and gradations. The tiny details require working very closely to the surface and minute trigger manipulations.

109. Instead of replacing a masking stencil to protect an area from overspray, it is often faster and more intuitive to use a hand-held shield like the Artool Big Shield FH-7 to shield an area from over-spray or to make a line crisper. A hard-edged line draws the eye and seems to make it closer to the viewer. This is important to note because it will add depth to your artwork.

110. Freehand detailing of the webbing.

111. The stencil is removed from the belly and magenta is freehand painted to render details.

112. Diamont White Pearl BC-110 is added into a mixing cup with the magenta. The pearl paint will give added visual dimension to the magenta. The pearlized magenta is airbrushed into the throat spines and gradated out into the blue of the spines.

113. I pull off the stencil that has covered the eye and cut the pupil out of it with an X-Acto knife. Then I clean the adhesive with 901.

114. I put a dark yellow into the airbrush and paint a portion of the iris.

115. I empty the color cup and add orange to the airbrush. The iris has orange painted into it. The pupil stencil is pulled up.

116. I put black in the airbrush. Now I can paint in the shadow of the dragon's eyebrow.

117. Next, I darken the yellow belly of the dragon to disguise the stenciled effect by airbrushing a soft gradation from the belly's edge into the black.

118. The stencils that cover the teeth and lower jaw are removed. Since these pieces have been adhered to the surface since the beginning of the project, there will be glue to clean away once they are pulled away. I save the stencils, because they will be cut apart during the painting process of the mouth and teeth.

Assorted Tips & Words of Wisdom

Always endeavor to give your customers good value for their money. Word of mouth is the best advertising you can get.

119. The stencils that correspond with the lower jaw and upper jaw are replaced to protect the areas from overspray when the mouth is sprayed. Masking paper extends the overspray protection beyond the stencils.

120. I mix a cream color to paint the base color of the teeth and mouth of the dragon. Notice that I am not just covering the area. I am leaving some areas darker than others to help to indicate shape of whatever I am painting. I am not looking to paint detail at this point. It is just a foundation color.

121. I will separate the lower teeth and side of the mouth from their stencil and use them as masks and shields to paint the mouth.

122. I have all the cut stencils arranged on a cutting mat that is on my lap. I position all of the pieces in their respective spots. Fitting the stencils together is similar to assembling a puzzle.

123. I mix an opaque dusty rose color to spray the base color for the tongue.

124. Next, I'll darken the dusty rose color by adding a bit of chocolate brown to deepen the flesh color. First, I place the tongue stencil in place.

125. The dark brown is sprayed to indicate the shadow of the tongue and teeth.

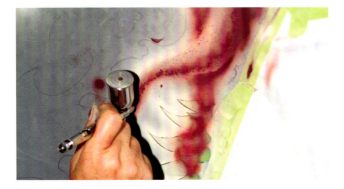

126. The tongue stencil is removed.

127. The stenciled edges are painted over with freehand dagger strokes to hide them.

128. I add some small dots to give the tongue some texture.

129. I pull up the stencils to expose the teeth.

130. I airbrush a dark yellow to jazz up the teeth.

Assorted Tips & Words of Wisdom

I cannot emphasize this enough..."Get a deposit on every job."

131. The airbrush is cleaned out, and the masking paper and stencils for the horns are removed. RM 901 Pre-Kleeno cleans away the adhesive residue left behind by the stencils.

132. The cream color is painted into the horns in order to provide a good base color to build details over. The main horn on the top of the head still has stencil material around it, so I don't need to worry about over-spray. Notice how I am mixing gradations with lines to define the shape of the main horn.

133. The horns on the side of the face have no stencil material surrounding them, so I need to hold the airbrush closer to the surface to paint in the edges before filling in the details in the center of the horn area. I paint long dagger strokes to indicate the roundness of the horn and give them some texture.

134. The same dark yellow that was used to paint the teeth is now used on the horns to further define their look. The top horn has the color sprayed from farther away because it is still masked. I keep the color light, so the details that I painted in the cream color show through the paint.

135. The facial horns require a different approach since they have no stencil material protecting their boundaries. The airbrush is held closer and the linear striations of the horn are airbrushed in freehand.

136. I mixed dark brown paint with gold to make a tan color. It is used to airbrush the tiny details of the horns. There is no mystery here — just a lot of dagger lines that connect to create the shapes and texture.

137. While this color is in the airbrush, I use it to paint more details into the teeth.

138. A deep dark reddish brown is mixed up using various opaque Diamont colors and is airbrushed to add detail and enhance the shadow of the tongue and horns, and to define their shapes. The side of the mouth is detailed to put it in proper perspective with its surroundings.

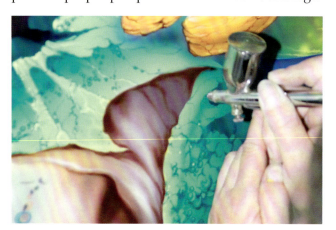

139. The airbrush is cleaned and all of the masking and stencil material is removed from the panel. When lifting the stencil material, always take care to pull up the stencil or tapes in a direction away from the painted edges to keep from peeling up paint. The surface is cleaned with 901 Pre-Kleeno.

140. Without all of the stencil and masking material, I get my first look at Draco. I see that the neck needs more turquoise. The color is loaded into the airbrush and I go to work free-handing the detail. I will not mask or shield at this point because I want the soft over-spray of the color to interact with the underlying color. This effect is not readily apparent until the panel is clear-coated. Only then will the pigments pop and the colors demonstrate the synergy of their marriage.

141. The same color is painted into the spines, scales, eye socket and throat.

142. Now is the time to contemplate the fire effect.

143. The base color for the fire is an opaque yellow-gold Diamont BC621 which appears almost orange. It is loaded into the color cup thinned to 2 parts reducer to 1 part paint. The fire effect in essence consists of building dagger strokes of various lengths and widths and melding them together.

144. The airbrush is cleaned and an opaque bright yellow is deposited into the color cup. It is painted to blend with the yellow-gold to define the fire licks. I use the Artool Big Shield to keep overspray from affecting the sharp edge of the mouth.

145. The same yellow is added into the eye and then is cleaned from the airbrush.

Assorted Tips & Words of Wisdom

Set your own prices based on the level of your competence and the local or regional market. Do not let the customer determine how much they will pay for your best work.

146. Transparent Yellow Carizzma with Sun-Fire Gold Powder is put into the airbrush and sprayed over the entire flaming area adding a special effect. I am not concerned with any of the transparent paint obscuring the black background — it won't happen. What will happen is a wonderful shimmer that will tie the flames into the background. Unfortunately, the effect won't be apparent until after the clear coat is applied. The color is evacuated from the gun.

147. Transparent Orange DB76 Carizzma is reduced to a 1-1 ratio with medium speed Diamont reducer and is added to the airbrush. It is sprayed over the flames starting at the point furthest from the dragon and fading the color as it intersects the bright yellow emitting from the dragon's mouth. Before painting, I clean the surface with the tack rag. As with the previous step, I want the overspray of the transparent color to interact with the special shimmering yellow on the black background. Airbrush trigger action is 0-10-0 from 12 inches away.

148. Fire effect is complete.

149. I reposition the stencils that protect the main horn on the top of the dragon's head and the spiny webbing from the dragon's right side so I can begin painting the nebula that is in the background.

150. Diamont Opaque White D 902 is over-reduced to a 2-1 ratio. This color will act as the good background for the nebula. I will start spraying the paint at 10 psi by adjusting the MAC valve on the airbrush. I will gradually reduce the air pressure to get larger dots in the spray pattern. I begin spraying at 10 psi. I use a soft gradation to create the oval shape. The pattern is rather grainy and pale. This step establishes the shape of the nebula. I spray large dots into the area with the same paint and air pressure to indicate mini galaxies.

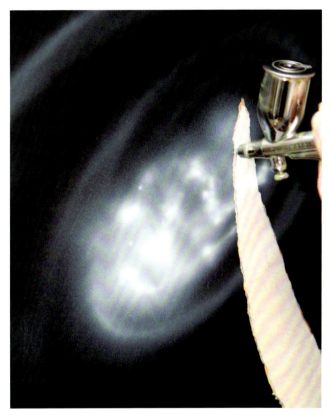

Assorted Tips & Words of Wisdom

Never stop learning. I constantly soak up any artistic inspiration available to keep my mind and my work fresh. Books, DVDs and other media have an impact on what I do and how I do it.

151. The MAC valve easily reduces the air pressure to 1 psi to render larger dots. I continue to paint over the galaxies until I am satisfied.

152. The opaque white is evacuated and cleaned from the airbrush. DB45 Teal Carizzma is put into the airbrush. The air pressure is quickly adjusted to 45 psi via the MAC valve on the airbrush. I spray a soft mist over the white stars and adjacent black space. In some places I paint darker than others so everything isn't the same.

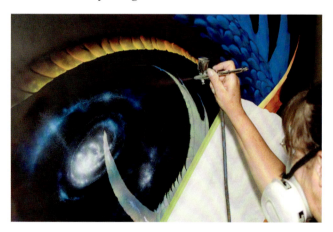

Assorted Tips & Words of Wisdom

The first layer of clearcoat applied over airbrushing should be sprayed as dry as possible and left to dry completely before additional wet coats are sprayed. If the first layer of clearcoat is sprayed too wet or takes too long to dry (possibly due to low shop temperature), it may cause the airbrushing to run. The tiniest airbrushed details will be the first to go.

153. Fuchsia is put into the airbrush and is sprayed over some of the teal stars and background to add some warm color.

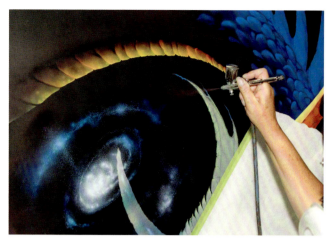

154. The masking is removed. Finished piece ready for clear coat.

above: Draco after clearcoat and polish — ready for display.

CHAPTER ELEVEN

Gallery

Ever since I started painting professionally, customers have sought out my services to help make their vehicle a "one of a kind." Many vehicle styling trends have come and gone during my 30 years of painting. When I was a novice, van murals were the rage. That fit my style perfectly since I prefer airbrushing artwork on vehicles as opposed to graphic designs.

After the van mural era exhausted itself in the late 70's and early 80's, geometric shapes and complex stripe designs were much in demand for automobiles. I did paint graphics and stripes quite a bit until I made a conscious decision to paint to my strengths. I successfully created a niche for myself by honing my mural painting skills to a level that set my work apart from the crowd. I also focused my marketing towards the motorcycle crowd because they seem to have the strongest demand for my type of painting.

Since I specialize in mural work, I strive to bring all my artistic tools to bear to create details and color effects that wow the viewer with incredible intricacies and astonishing color vibrancy. The following examples illustrate my signature style.

above: A radically hot Camaro

left: Pamela Shanteau with one of her infamous flaming skulls

Assorted Tips & Words of Wisdom

The most effective way to market your services is to display your work at as many vehicle-related events as you can. Be prepared to meet and greet your prospective customers so they will go away with the confidence to trust their "ride" in your hands.

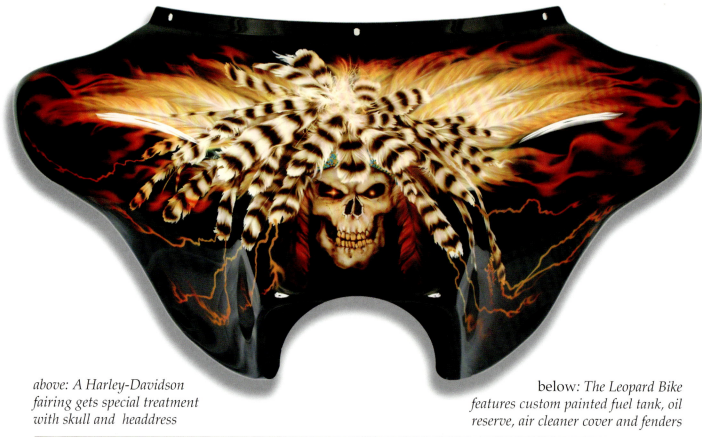

above: A Harley-Davidson fairing gets special treatment with skull and headdress

below: The Leopard Bike features custom painted fuel tank, oil reserve, air cleaner cover and fenders

right: A closer look at the Leopard Bike's tank

Motorcycle Tanks

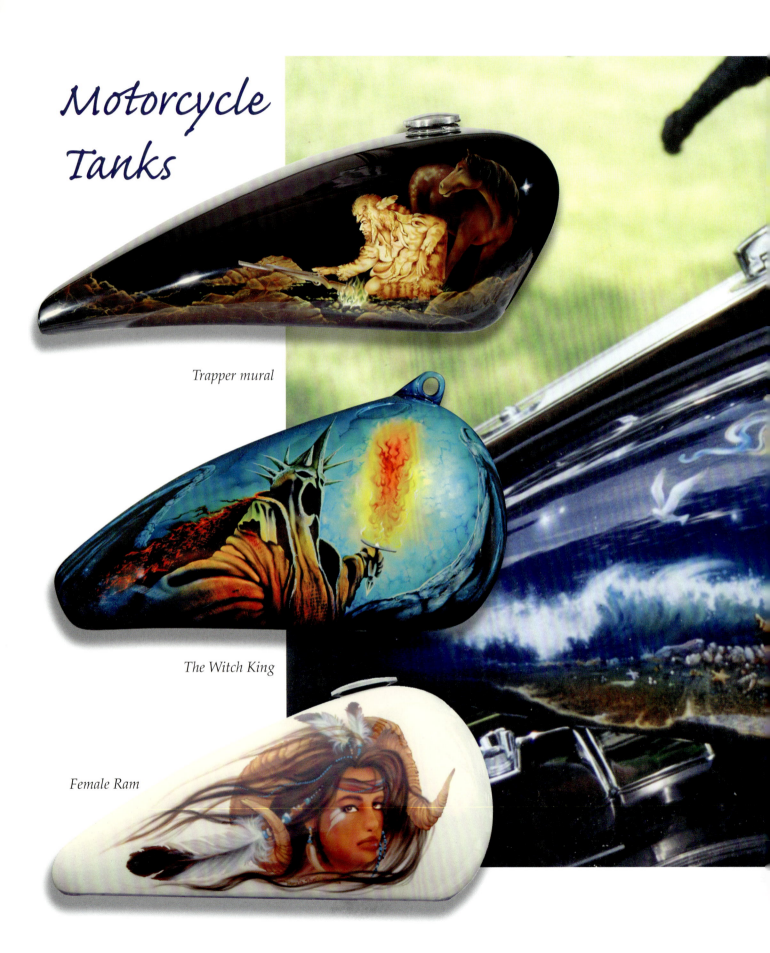

Trapper mural

The Witch King

Female Ram

above: Wiccan Priestess on motorcycle tank

left: Realistic flames on helmet – circa 1984

above: Pamela shows her kinder/gentler side as she completes a large mural on an RV

left: Realistic fire and skulls continue strong among the motorcycle community as a creative form of expression

right: Eagles and flags on American iron are always a popular combination

CHAPTER TWELVE

Other Works

Custom painting on vehicles is a very big part of our business, now more than ever. Many people don't realize it, but at one time, commercial illustration was a much bigger part of my business. I worked mainly in the fantasy role-playing industry for a number of game producers. The art eventually ended up on some collectable playing card or turned up as a page in some gaming literature like Dragon Magazine. As the nature of that industry changed, I divested myself from that part of my business to concentrate on my first love, customizing autos and motorcycles.

I still instruct fine art and illustration techniques at art shows around the country, and occasionally I still get asked to do a painting for a commercial endeavor or an individual. When that happens, I prefer to paint on a surface called Claybord. Claybord is a hard-pressed board with a clay coating on one side. It is manufactured by Ampersand Art Products in Austin Texas. The clay surface is perfect for airbrushing. It offers many ways to manipulate its painted surface to create awesome details and save time. Some of my Claybord painting techniques translate directly to my auto and cycle painting methods.

Here are some examples of my fine art and commercial work. All are on Claybord.

above: My working studio. This is where I do my lay-outs, commercial illustration or fine art paintings.

left: Leopard on 30" x 40" Claybord. Paints; Glasurit automotive base coats with RM Carizzma automotive polyester dyes. Clear-coated with Glasurit automotive PolyUrethane paint.

above: Violet Moon – 30" x 40" Claybord – Paints: Medea Com-Art & Holbein Aero-Flash acrylics
left: Delmer – 30" x 40" Claybord Panel – Paints: Medea Com-Art Colours & Holbein Aero-Flash acrylics

OTHER WORKS

above: A 4'x 6' Claybord panel that was painted for a trading card that was part of an oriental role-playing game system.

far left: Serena
16"x 20" Claybord panel
There is no white paint on this piece at all. All whites and highlights were created by erasing paint to expose the substrate.

left: Selene's Thyme
16" x 20" Claybord Panel
One of the few paintings that I have done that did not use some sort of reference. This one came straight from my brain.

right: Lilli Pearl
16" x 20" Claybord panel
Donn photographed a she-vampire in Milwaukee and I adapted the image to the one you see here.

Glossary of Terms

Accelerator — Additive that speeds up the dry time for paint.

Adhesion Promoter — Sprays over-cured paint to chemically enhance bonding of subsequent paint coats.

Base Coat — The colored paint that is sandwiched between the primer and the clearcoat.

Block Sanding — A rubber block is wrapped with sand paper to ensure even pressure over the entire surface of the paper while working.

Blushing — Milky haze that appears in the clearcoat.

Body Filler / Bondo — Polyester putty that is used to repair minor substrate imperfections.

Buffing — Polishing compounds with various abrasive qualities are applied to the final clearcoat. Normally this is done with the aid of an electric buffer, which spins the soft rubber pads with fabric covers or foam pads that apply the polishing compounds.

Burn Through — This happens if a clear-coated finish is buffed too aggressively. The underlying color coat will be exposed and the area will need to be re-cleared.

Candy Paints — Generic term used for any transparent automotive paint. Candy paint colors are sprayed in light coats to build the color value with control. More coats equal deeper candy color. Candy paint color is affected by its underlying base color. Spraying candy red over a blue base would make the vehicle take on a purple hue.

Catalyst — Additive that causes a paint to harden.

Checking — Fine cracks in the clear coat. It is most often caused by over application of the clearcoat.

Clearcoat — Enamel, urethane or lacquer paint that contains no pigments. It protects and enhances the base coat.

Crazing — Thin cracks in the base coat.

Dagger Stroke — An airbrushed line of any width with tapered ends that end in a fine point.

Dry Sanding — Use of automotive sand paper to remove paint or to abrade a painted surface to a desired coarseness. Dry sanding paper grits vary from course to fine.

Fish Eye — Crater-like blemish in the paint that resembles the fish's eye. These can be caused by oily or silicone contaminates in the air, or by not cleaning the surface with a degreaser/cleaner before painting.

Flash Time — Period of time you must wait to spray another coat of paint over a freshly sprayed one. All of the solvents must evaporate from the previous coat before another can be sprayed.

Flex Agent — Added to paint to make it pliable. Used when painting over rubber or soft plastics.

Flow — How well wet paint levels itself on the surface after application.

Flip Paints — Pigments that have tiny particles suspended in them that reflect light in such a way that the paint appears to change or "flip" to another color when viewed from different angles

Ghosting — Ghost flames and other types of ghosted graphics or artwork are accomplished by burying the art or graphic under multiple coats of transparent paint. Two factors affect how "ghosted "something is. The first is the number of overlaying transparent coats of paint that go over the art. More layers equal a deeper ghost effect. The second factor that affects the level of "ghosting" is how the color of the graphics contrasts with the other paint colors in the scheme. Subtle differences between the base color and that of the art or graphic (light orange on middle orange or a middle gray on black) ghost easier than boldly contrasting colors.

Glazing Compound — Super-fine polishing compound that produces maximum gloss in the clear coat.

Gradation — Painted area that blends from light to dark with no apparent lines or blotches in the pattern. I also use the term to describe how to airbrush paint into the exposed areas of stencils to avoid building paint up against the stencil's edge.

HVLP — Acronym for High Volume Low Pressure spray systems.

Isocyanates — Toxic chemical compound found in many paint catalysts.

Lacquer Thinner — Used to clean air guns and other tools used in the painting process.

Masking — Any tape, plastic or paper that is used to protect an area from the over-spray that air painting creates.

Metallics and Micas — Tiny colored flakes that are added to the color coat to add a glitter effect.

MSDS Sheets — Material Safety and Data Sheets. Available from the vendor for all paints that contain hazardous material.

Negative Stencil — The part of the stencil that abuts or is around the area that is being painted when stenciling.

Orange Peel — Textured finish in the dried clear coat that resembles an orange peel. It is usually caused by poor spraying method or a poorly adjusted spray gun.

OSHA — Occupational Safety and Health Administration. Sets guidelines and regulates safety in the workplace.

Paint Build — Indicates the thickness of the paint or its profile.

Peeling — Sheets of paint peel from the surface due to poor bond to the underlying layer of paint.

PEL — Permissible Exposure Limit. Stated on MSDS, lets you know how long you can be exposed to the chemicals in the paint.

Pigment — The ingredient that makes the color in a paint.

Polyisocyanates — Toxic chemical compound found in many paint catalysts.

Positive Stencil — The part of any stencil that corresponds to the area that is being painted. This part of the stencil is usually cut apart into many mini-stencils as I airbrush in the details of the image. The freshly cut mini stencils become new sets of mini positive and negative stencils. In a complicated piece of artwork, stencil pieces might serve double duty as positive or negative counterparts to each other.

Glossary of Terms, con't.

Pot Life — Indicates how long paint will be spray-able if it has been catalyzed.

Pre-Kleener — Wax and grease removing solvent that evaporates very fast once it is wiped onto the surface. It can be used to remove any foreign matter including adhesives from a painted surface.

Primer — Paint that creates the bond between the substrate and the color coat. It also fills in small blemishes.

Product Information Sheets — State mixing ratios, dry times and other relevant information for the paint.

Reducer — A solvent that thins the paint to make it suitable for spraying. Available in fast, medium and slow evaporation rates to match ambient conditions.

Runs — Sags or drips in the paint. Usually caused by over application or cold temperatures in the paint shop.

Scallops — Straight tapering graphics that are painted on a vehicle in the style of flames.

Sand Scratch Swelling — Caused when an old paint finish is sanded and the sand marks swell up when the solvents in the next coat of paint are introduced to the finish.

Scuff Pad — Abrasive pad made of plastic fibers that is flexible and slightly abrasive. It is best suited for sanding edges, rivets and other situations where it is easy to burn through the base coat or clearcoat with regular sanding papers.

Sgraffito — The fine art technique of removing an applied pigment and selectively exposing the underlying color or substrate. This method renders details, highlights or color gradations by removing paint not applying it.

Shield — Hand-held object that is used to protect an area from paint overspray or is used to create a shape by airbrushing paint around its outline or any interior edges it might have.

Single Stage Paint — Requires no clearcoat.

Solvents — Chemical additives that thin the paint so it can be sprayed effectively.

Substrate — The bare surface that you are painting on. It might be aluminum, steel, fiberglass, Kevlar or any other surface.

Tack Cloth — Cloths with a sticky coating that removes lint and dust from a surface prior to painting.

Two Part Paint — Requires a catalyst to be mixed into the paint so it will dry.

VOC — Volatile Organic Compounds are dispersed into the environment from the solvents used to reduce or thin the paint.

Wet Sanding — Use of automotive sand paper in conjunction with clean water to either smooth a coat of paint before the buffing process takes place or to scuff-up a painted surface so it has some tooth for additional coats of paint or to prepare for custom airbrush applications.

Trouble-Shooting

The most important part of trouble-shooting is avoiding trouble in the first place. To work properly, an airbrush must be sufficiently cleaned after every use. Cleaning usually involves flushing the paint reservoir and paint path through the airbrush with the appropriate solvent until all paint residues are eliminated. This includes the interior of the paint nozzle and the point where the paint nozzle seals against the body of the airbrush. After the cleansing process, the paint needle can be very lightly coated with petroleum jelly or lightweight oil for storage. Be sure to wipe the needle clean before painting again.

Problem:	Solution:
• Paint will not spray	• Make sure air source is connected and working. Check airlines for restriction. Clean paint nozzle. Make sure regulator is adjusted properly. Make sure paint is in the airbrush.
• Paint sprays when only clean air should be exiting the airbrush	• Check to see if the paint needle is positioned correctly. Clean the paint nozzle. If these two fixes do not work, the paint nozzle is most likely damaged slightly. In that case replacement of the paint nozzle is the only fix available.
• Paint sprays from the airbrush intermittently or sprays with a machine-gun effect.	• Clean the area on the airbrush that the paint nozzle seats against. This seal must be perfect or the airbrush will malfunction.
• Airbrush makes bubbles in the color cup or color bottle	• Clean the area on the airbrush that the paint nozzle seats against. Make sure that the paint nozzle and needle guard have no restrictions.
• Trigger does not return to the up position once it has been depressed	• Clean the rubber seal at the top of the air valve in the stem of the airbrush with airbrush cleaner. Lubricate and condition the o-ring with a bit of petroleum jelly. If this method does not help, the entire air valve may have been gummed up by paint or dirty reducer intrusion, disassembly and soaking the valve in reducer may help, otherwise the air valve may need to be replaced.
• Paint hangs up on the tip of the airbrush needle	• Paint may need to be thinned or reduced to a greater degree. Paint needle may be bent at the tip. Poor trigger control technique allows the paint to build up.
• Paint sprays unevenly	• Check condition of paint needle and paint nozzle. If either is damaged, you must replace them. Make sure no foreign materials such as dried paint flakes are in the paint nozzle clogging its orifice.

Resources

3M Global Headquarters

Postal Address:
3M Corporate Headquarters
3M Center
St. Paul, MN 55144-1000

Phone: 1-888-3M HELPS
(1-888-364-3577)

online at www.3M.com

Artool, Inc.

Postal Address:
Artool Products Company
P.O. Box 14397
Portland, OR 97293

Phone: (503) 253-7308
Fax: (503) 253-0721

online at www.ArtoolProducts.com

ANEST IWATA, USA, Inc.

Postal Address:
Anest Iwata, USA, Inc.
9920 Windisch Rd
West Chester, OH 45069

Phone: (513) 755-3100
Fax: (513) 755-0888

online at www.anestiwata.com

BASF

Postal Address:
BASF Group - North America
BASF Corporation
100 Campus Drive
Florham Park, N.J. 07932
USA

Phone: (973) 245-6077
Fax: (973) 245-6714

online at www.BASF.com

Iwata-Medea, Inc.

Postal Address:
Iwata-Medea Airbrush Products
P.O. Box 14397
Portland, OR 97293

Phone: (503) 253-7308
Fax: (503) 253-0721

online at www.IwataAirbrush.com

House of Kolor

Postal Address:
House of Kolor, Inc.
2521 27th South
Minneapolis, MN 55406

Phone: (601) 798-6147
Fax: (601) 798-6147

online at www.houseofkolor.com

Index

Additives *20, 27, 28, 156*
Air Compressor *12-16, 31, 46*
Airbrush Choices *31-33*
Air Gun Holder *23,24*
Anest Iwata *12, 31-33*
Artool *22-25, 62, 75, 76, 129, 132, 135*
Auto Air *27*
Auto-Painting Accessories *19*
Automotive Paints *27-29, 42*

Base Coat *20, 27-29, 33, 45, 83, 85, 99*
Bottles, Airbrush *21, 33*

Catalysts *28, 29*
CFM *31*
Claybord *103, 149*
Cleaning Kits *22*
Clearcoat *11, 14, 15, 17, 20, 27-29, 33, 44, 45, 48, 49, 61, 87, 103, 128, 136, 138*
Color Coat *45, 47-49*
Compressor *12-16, 31, 46*
Cutting Rail *22*

Drafting Film *22, 23, 25, 51-54, 57, 58, 61, 78, 79, 91, 92, 106, 114*
DuPont *27*

Exhaust Fan *12, 13, 15, 16*

Fiberglass Eraser *103*
Fire Safety *16*

Gravity-Feed *31, 32*

Hand Cleaner *25*
HAPS *29*
Hardeners *28*
House of Kolor *27, 158*
HVLP - *High Volume-Low Pressure* *12, 15, 31, 51*

Isocyanides *29*
Iwata *6, 12, 13, 15, 31-33, 56, 94, 102, 113, 158*

Jobber *11, 23*
Lighting *13, 15, 16*

MAC Valve — *Micro Air Control* *32, 65, 67, 102, 137, 138*
Masking Machine *19*
Masking Paper *19, 25, 51, 56, 62, 69, 70, 72, 73, 75, 81, 108, 109, 125, 127, 131, 133*
Masking Tape *19, 21, 51, 56, 69, 81, 92, 93, 103, 107-109*
Measuring Cups *20*
Mixing Ratio *27*

Paint
~ Additives *20, 27, 28, 156*
~ Enamel *28, 29*
~ Laquer *28, 29*
~ Polyester *29, 61*
~ Reducers *14, 16, 27, 28, 46, 95, 128, 135, 136, 157*
~ Solvent-Based *29*
~ Urethane-Based *28, 29*
~ Waterborne *29*
Paint Filter *20*
Painter Safety *43, 16*
Plastic Sheeting *25, 51*
Pneumatic Sanders *17*
PPG *27*
Primer *11, 14, 15, 17, 33, 44, 45, 47, 48*
Projector *25, 61, 106*

Quick-Disconnect Fittings *13, 20*

Reducers *14, 16, 27, 28, 46, 95, 128, 135, 136, 157*
Regulator *13, 16, 20, 46, 157*
R+M *27*

Sandpaper *19, 28, 44, 87*
Self Healing Cutting Mat *22, 131*
SEM *27*
SEMA *105*
Shields *22-24, 51-53, 57, 93, 131, 132*
Side-Feed *21, 31, 32*
Sikkens *27*

Siphon-Feed *21, 31, 33*
Solvents *14, 20, 22, 28, 29*
Solvent-Proof Gloves *14, 16*
Stencil Burner *23, 53, 57, 79, 80, 92, 95, 100, 106, 112, 114, 115, 118, 120, 127*
Stir Sticks *20*
Stretch Mask *23, 52, 62, 63, 65, 67*

Tack Rag *21, 45, 47, 85, 87, 113, 119, 121, 136*
Tape
~ Masking *19, 21, 51, 56, 69, 81, 92, 93, 103, 107-109*
~ Transfer *24, 25, 51, 52, 71, 72, 75*
Tech Sheet *27, 46, 49*
Trouble Shooting *155*

Ultra Mask *25*

Valspar *27*
Vinyl Plotter/Cutter *24, 25, 52, 61, 70, 74*
VOCs *29*

Wet-Sanding *15, 19, 45, 49, 61, 87*
Work Tables/Surfaces *13, 14, 16*
Workspace *11, 12, 14, 15, 23, 51*

X-Acto Knives *22, 51, 53, 62, 71, 74, 79, 95, 107, 112, 118, 130*